RELIGION IN HISTORY

AND IN

MODERN LIFE

"*Nevertheless it is open to serious question, which I leave to the reader's pondering, whether, among national manufactures, that of souls of a good quality may not at last turn out a quite leadingly lucrative one? Nay, in some far-away and yet undreamt-of hour, I can even imagine that England may cast all thoughts of possessing wealth back to the barbaric nations among whom they first arose, and that, while the sands of the Indus and adamant of Golconda may yet stiffen the housings of the charger, and flash from the turban of the slave, she, as a Christian mother, may at last attain to the virtues and the treasures of a heathen one, and be able to lead forth her sons, saying · 'These are my jewels'*"—Ruskin, "Unto this Last," II.

"*The people are the most important element [in a country]; the spirits of the land and grain are the next; the ruler is the lightest.*

"*Therefore, to gain the peasantry is the way to become the son of Heaven, to gain the son of Heaven is the way to become the prince of a state, to gain the prince of a state is the way to become a great officer*"—"Mencius," Book VII, Part II, Chapter XIV

> "*It was the lesson of our great ancestor —
> The people should be cherished,
> And not looked down upon
> The people are the root of a country,
> The root firm, the country is tranquil*
>
> . . . . .
>
> *Should dissatisfaction be waited for till it appears?
> Before it is seen, it should be guarded against
> In my dealings with the millions of the people,
> I should feel as much anxiety as if I were driving six
> horses with rotten reins*"
>
> "The Shû King," Part I, Book III

"*Nothing is more becoming to him who governs than to despise no man and not show arrogance, but to preside over all with equal care*"—Epictetus, "Encheiridion," CXXXII.

RELIGION IN HISTORY

AND IN

MODERN LIFE

TOGETHER WITH AN ESSAY ON THE CHURCH
AND THE WORKING CLASSES

BY

A. M. FAIRBAIRN, D.D.
PRINCIPAL OF MANSFIELD COLLEGE, OXFORD

NINTH THOUSAND

New York
A. D. F. RANDOLPH AND CO.
182 FIFTH AVENUE

MDCCCXCV

Wipf and Stock Publishers
199 W 8th Ave, Suite 3
Eugene, OR 97401

Religion in History and in Modern Life
Together With an Essay on the Church and the Working Classes
By Fairbairn, A. M.
Softcover ISBN-13: 978-1-7252-9662-6
Hardcover ISBN-13: 978-1-7252-9663-3
eBook ISBN-13: 978-1-7252-9664-0
Publication date 1/6/2021
Previously published by A. D. F. Randolph and Co., 1895

This edition is a scanned facsimile of
the original edition published in 1895.

"*Quench not the Spirit, despise not prophesyings, prove all things, hold fast that which is good, abstain from every form of evil.*
"*And the God of peace himself sanctify you wholly, and may your spirit and soul and body be preserved entire, without blame, at the coming of our Lord Jesus Christ.*"—1 Thess v 19-23

PREFACE

THIS little book is republished in response to much friendly pressure which has come from many sides. While it has been revised throughout, and in certain places expanded, yet expansion has not been found possible where it was most needed —in the concluding lecture. But this is the less regretted as the book is not an essay in what it is the fashion to call Christian Economics, but rather a discussion as to the nature and action of the Christian Religion as it has revealed and fulfilled itself in history. Abstract economics, even though deduced from the Sermon on the Mount, are more likely to be ingenious than either relevant to the original or practicable in the present, ideals that do not so much produce realities as become apologies for their absence. A man who is a good exegete but an inexperienced economist, is no more able to apply the New Testament to our social and industrial problems, than the man who is an expert economist but a stranger to the New Testament. To make knowledge of the one subject a reason for attempting to write on both, is simply to show how foolish a reasonable man may be, for it is nowhere so hard to think truly and speak wisely as in the application of simple maxims to complex problems. This, of course, does not mean either that the ethics of Christ ought not, or that they cannot be applied to modern economics; on the contrary, the whole argument of the book is governed by the conviction that they ought to be so applied, and that the whole past life of the Christian Religion has been a series of efforts to embody itself in a higher social and economical order. From these efforts the religion cannot desist, and against the hindrances to them it must for evermore contend. But then in order to the success of this contention the churches must see clearly that they may strike boldly; to hit blindly is only to inflict damage all round.

Now, the author is not a student of economics—in this region he feels rather than sees, but he is a student of the history of religion, and he feels more able to define the duty and function of religion in the present when he comes to it through the experience of the past. And this is all he really professes to do, but even so, this is no little or insignificant thing to attempt. In studying the history and the action of Christian ideas, we move in the region of the actual, and learn through what the religion has done, what it is capable of doing, what it has failed to do, why it has failed to do it, and what it ought now to set itself to accomplish. The historical thus becomes a most practical discussion, and forms a necessary and sobering introduction to every attempt to deal either critically or constructively with the economic functions of the Christian religion. But the author has no wish to escape, under the disguise of an historical discussion, the grave responsibility which lies upon every Christian teacher to apply his religion to the present. His sense of this responsibility, within the limits defined by the origin and purpose of the lectures, is partially expressed in the essay on " The Church and the Working Classes." Without this recognition of duty he could not have allowed this book to go forth in a new edition.

Perhaps it may be as well to recall the original purpose of the *Lectures* which form the body of the book. The author was then resident in the neighbourhood of Bradford, and he volunteered to address the working men of the town on " Religion in History," expressly through the press inviting them to attend. His purpose was thus stated in the Preface to the First Edition :—

" The reasons which induced me to take so

unusual a step had a twofold source ; first, the strong conviction of what Religion is, and what it ought to do ; and, secondly, the feeling that it is the duty of the special student to become, as far as possible, a teacher of the people, especially in matters where the people so much need instruction, and where instruction is so necessary to their highest good. Our hard-worked ministers and clergy have quite enough to do without attempting labour of this kind ; yet it is labour that ought to be done. The ordinary pulpit leaves many questions undiscussed, and the ordinary congregation does not desire or require their discussion ; yet they are questions everywhere anxiously debated by earnest and most excellent men. It is easy, through the press, to reach the cultivated and leisured classes ; it is not so easy, indeed to many it is quite impossible, to reach the industrial classes through it. Yet these latter are often the more susceptible, with natures more open to conviction, more fully convinced, if convinced at all. Some things that had recently happened within my own experience, made me very vividly aware of the peculiar forms our religious problems and difficulties assume among our working men, and this discovery led to the feeling of obligation that resulted in the delivery of these *Lectures*. I felt bound, as a student and teacher of the Christian religion, to speak to my fellow townsmen, especially those of the industrial classes, concerning questions they were discussing and honestly trying to understand.

" The Lectures were determined alike as to matter and form by their purpose. They are not apologetic in the customary sense, but I hope they are something better, because more relevant to the actual state of mind of the persons addressed. It will be but just if they are judged according to their real intention and scope, and in no respect as a polemical and controversial endeavour."

December 10, 1893.

"*The King said to his people* '*The good in you I will not dare to keep concealed, and for the evil in me I will not dare to forgive myself I will examine these things in harmony with the mind of God When guilt is found anywhere in you who occupy the myriad regions, let it rest on me, the One man. When guilt is found in me, the One man, it shall not attach to you who occupy the myriad regions.*'"—"The Shû King," Part iv., Book iii., Part 3

"*Heaven loves the people, and the sovereign should reverently carry out (this mind of) Heaven*"—Ib., Part v., Book i., § 2.

"*The ancients have said, 'He who soothes us is our sovereign; he who oppresses us is our enemy*'"—Ib., Part v, Book i, § 3

"*A state exists for the sake of a good life, and not for the sake of life only if life only were the object, slaves and brute animals might form a state, but they cannot, for they have no share in happiness or in a life of free choice . Whence it may be further inferred that virtue must be the serious care of a state which truly deserves the name. for (without this ethical end) the community becomes a mere alliance which differs only in place from alliances of which the members live apart, and law is only a convention, 'a surety to one another of justice,' as the sophist Lycophron says, and has no real power to make the citizens good and just.*"—Aristotle, "Politics," Book i., § 9.

"*It has been well said that 'he who has never learned to obey cannot be a good commander' The two are not the same, but the good citizen ought to be capable of both, he should know how to govern like a freeman, and how to obey like a freeman—these are the virtues of a citizen*"—Ib., Book iii., § 4

"*Two principles are characteristic of democracy, the government of the majority and freedom. Men think that what is just is equal, and that equality is the supremacy of the popular will, and that freedom and equality mean the doing what a man likes In such democracies every one lives as he pleases, or in the words of Euripides, 'according to his fancy.' But this is all wrong, men should not think it slavery to live according to the rule of the constitution, for it is their salvation*"—Ib., Book v., § 9

"*Neither is a horse elated nor proud of his manger and trappings and coverings, nor a bird of his little shreds of cloth or of his nest · but both of them are proud of their swiftness, one proud of the swiftness of the feet, and the other of the wings Do you also, then, not be greatly proud of your food and dress, and, in short, of any external things, but be proud of your integrity and good deeds* (εὐποιία)"—Epictetus, "Encheiridion," xxvi.

CONTENTS

THE CHURCH AND THE WORKING CLASSES

1 ITS CHANGED ATTITUDE TO THE WORKING CLASSES—
PAGE
 The Religious Causes of this Change and its Forms   3
 Its Effects on Different Classes of Society .   5
 The New and Practical Interest in Labour Questions   8

2 THE ATTITUDE OF THE MEN TO THE CHURCHES—
 Less Change in their Attitude .   11
 The Alienation from the Churches   13

3 CAUSES, APPARENT AND REAL, OF ALIENATION—
 Distrust of the Churches rather than Disbelief at Work   16
 The Loss of Adaptation by the Church to its Environment   20

4 INFLUENCE OF THE POLITICAL DEVELOPMENT—
 The Organic Relation of Political and Religious Thought .   23
 The Conflict of the New Ideas and the Old Order in the French Revolution   26
 The New Ideas and the English Churches   27
 The Church to-day must be as the State is   30

5 INFLUENCE OF SOCIETY AND THE SOCIAL SPIRIT—
 Divisive Social Tendencies   32
 Their Action within the Churches, how to be checked   34

6. INFLUENCE OF THE INDUSTRIAL DEVELOPMENT—

	PAGE
Its Hostility to the Cultivation of the Religious Spirit .	37
The Remedies and the Counteragencies required . .	39

7. INFLUENCE OF THE INTELLECTUAL MOVEMENT—

The Literature and Educative Forces of Modern Life . . 42
Religious Education as it is and as it ought to be . . 47

8. THE CONCILIATION OF THE ALIENATED—

The Church to be faithful to its Mission . . 50
Its Influence on the Mind, the Life, and the Home . . 54

9 URGENCY OF THE NEED—

The Modern Democracy . our Last Reserves . . . 58
The Rulers must be ruled 60

LECTURE I

WHAT IS RELIGION ?

CLEARNESS IN OUR IDEA OF IT NECESSARY	65
1. THE RELATION OF THE CHURCHES TO IT . . .	67
2. IT IS UNIVERSAL AND NATURAL TO MAN	72
3. PHILOSOPHICAL EXPLANATIONS . . .	78
4 ITS HIGHEST CONCEPTION DETERMINES ITS CHARACTER .	87
BY IT THE ENDS OF GOD REALIZED THROUGH MAN .	89

LECTURE II

THE PLACE AND SIGNIFICANCE OF THE OLD TESTAMENT IN RELIGION

	PAGE
RESTATEMENT OF TEMPER AND PRINCIPLES OF INQUIRY	94
1. THE SCIENTIFIC METHOD OF STUDY	97
POPULAR DIFFICULTIES CONCERNING THE BIBLE	102
2. THE OLD TESTAMENT THE HISTORY OF A RELIGION	106
THE NAME AND CHARACTER OF GOD	110
THE HEBREW PEOPLE AND ITS FAITH	114
3. THE REGULATIVE AND ORGANIZING POWER OF A GREAT CONCEPTION	117
THE MOSAIC IDEAL OF RELIGION	120
4. ITS NOTION OF MAN AS MORAL	123
AND OF THE STATE AS THE SAME	125
5. THE LAW IN OTHER RELATIONS	127
THE SPIRITUAL AND MORAL WEALTH OF THE OLD TESTAMENT	132

LECTURE III

THE PLACE AND SIGNIFICANCE OF THE NEW TESTAMENT IN RELIGION

1. THE OLD TESTAMENT THE PRIMARY SOURCE OF OUR MORAL IDEALS IN RELIGION	136
THE NEW TESTAMENT INHERITS AND UNIVERSALIZES THESE	140
2. CHRIST AND THE TRADITIONAL IDEALS OF HIS DAY	143
HIS OWN IDEAL	145

	PAGE
THE KINGDOM OF GOD, ITS EMBODIMENT	147
3. THE CHRISTIAN IDEAS OF GOD AND OF MAN	150
THESE IDEAS, HOW RELATED IN CHRISTIANITY AND IN OTHER RELIGIONS	156
4. THE UNITY OF MANKIND IN THE CITY OF GOD	159
CHRISTIANITY A RELIGION OF REDEMPTION	165
5. CHRIST'S INFLUENCE ON PERSONALITIES	168
THE REDEEMER AND LEADER OF PROGRESS	172

LECTURE IV

THE CHRISTIAN RELIGION IN THE FIRST FIFTEEN CENTURIES OF ITS EXISTENCE

THE SCOPE AND PURPOSE OF THE LECTURE	175
1. THE DISTINCTIVE NOTES OF EARLY CHRISTIANITY	179
2. THE INFLUENCE OF CERTAIN OLD PAGAN AND JUDAIC IDEAS	190
3. THE EFFECT OF CHRISTIAN IDEAS ON THE INDUSTRIAL AND SOCIAL SYSTEM OF ANCIENT ROME	194
4. THE ACTION OF THE CHRISTIAN FAITH ON THE LIFE OF MAN	201

LECTURE V

THE CHRISTIAN RELIGION IN MODERN EUROPE

THE ENERGY AND THE PAIN OF MODERN LIFE	206
1. THE POWER OF THE CHURCHES AND THE STRENGTH OF FAITH	208
2. THE RENAISSANCE AND THE REFORMATION	213
3 THE INFLUENCE OF CALVIN	217

		PAGE
4. Liberty, Political and Religious, whence sprung .		222
Its Source in the Religion of Christ .		226
Equality .		232
Fraternity .		233
The Ameliorative Forces of Modern Society . .		235

LECTURE VI

The Christian Religion in Modern Life

The Province of Religion		237
1. Ultimate Ideas and the Organization of Societies	.	239
The Evolution of the Modern Christian Ideal of Humanity .		243
2 Various Ancient and Modern Ideas compared herewith		245
The Architectonic Power of the Christian Religion		252
3. Its Application in Various Departments of Life		254
The Ideal of Christ our Hope for the Future .	.	270

"Behold my servant, whom I uphold, my chosen, in whom my soul delighteth: I have put my spirit upon him, he shall bring forth judgement to the Gentiles. He shall not cry, nor lift up, nor cause his voice to be heard in the street. A bruised reed shall he not break, and the smoking flax shall he not quench: he shall bring forth judgement in truth. He shall not fail nor be discouraged, till he have set judgement in the earth, and the isles shall wait for his law."—Isaiah xlii. 1-4

"And he came to Nazareth, where he had been brought up · and he entered, as his custom was, into the synagogue on the sabbath day, and stood up to read. And there was delivered unto him the book of the prophet Isaiah And he opened the book, and found the place where it was written,

> *'The Spirit of the Lord is upon me,*
> *Because he anointed me to preach good tidings to the poor.*
> *He hath sent me to proclaim release to the captives,*
> *And recovering of sight to the blind,*
> *To set at liberty them that are bruised,*
> *To proclaim the acceptable year of the Lord.'"*
>
> St Luke iv 16-19

"For when the ear heard me, then it blessed me,
And when the eye saw me, it gave witness unto me
Because I delivered the poor that cried,
The fatherless also, that had none to help him.
The blessing of him that was ready to perish came upon me
And I caused the widow's heart to sing for joy
I put on righteousness, and it clothed me
My justice was as a robe and a diadem.
I was eyes to the blind,
And feet was I to the lame
I was a father to the needy
And the cause of him that I knew not I searched out "

Job xxix. 11-16

"Render to no man evil for evil. Take thought for things honourable in the sight of all men If it be possible, as much as in you lieth, be at peace with all men "—Romans xii 17, 18

THE CHURCH AND THE WORKING CLASSES

"*The Working Classes cannot any longer go on without government, without being actually guided and governed, England cannot subsist in peace till, by some means or other, some guidance and government for them is found*"—Carlyle, "Chartism," Chapter vi.

"*There is not a hamlet where poor peasants congregate, but, by one means and another, a Church-Apparatus has been got together,—roofed edifice, with revenues and belfries, pulpit, reading-desk, with Books and Methods · possibility, in short, and strict prescription, That a man stand there and speak of spiritual things to men. It is beautiful,—even in its great obscuration and decadence, it is among the beautifulest, most touching objects one sees on the Earth. This Speaking Man has indeed, in these times, wandered terribly from the point, has, alas, as it were, totally lost sight of the point. yet, at bottom, whom have we to compare with him? Of all public functionaries boarded and lodged on the Industry of Modern Europe, is there one worthier of the board he has? A man even professing, and never so languidly making still some endeavour, to save the souls of men contrast him with a man professing to do little but shoot the partridges of men! I wish he could find the point again, this Speaking One, and stick to it with tenacity, with deadly energy, for there is need of him yet! The Speaking Function, this of Truth coming to us with a living voice, nay in a living shape, and as a concrete practical exemplar this, with all our Writing and Printing Functions, has a perennial place. Could he but find the point again,—take the old spectacles off his nose, and looking up discover, almost in contact with him, what the* real *Satanas and soul-devouring, world-devouring* Devil, *now is! Original Sin and suchlike are bad enough, I doubt not. but distilled Gin, dark Ignorance, Stupidity, dark Corn-Law, Bastille and Company, what are they!* Will *he discover our new real Satan, whom he has to fight, or go on droning through his old nose-spectacles about old extinct Satans, and never see the real one, till he* feel *him at his own throat and ours? That is a question, for the world!*"—Carlyle, "Past and Present," Book iv, Chapter i.

THE CHURCH AND THE WORKING CLASSES

I

CHANGED ATTITUDE TO THE WORKING CLASSES

IT is now almost ten years since these Lectures were delivered, and this period is remarkable for the growth in all religious societies of a new feeling for our workmen, and of responsibility in connexion with their special problems.

1. The causes and forms of this latest and most hopeful outgrowth of the Christian conscience are many and most varied. The generous and trustful humanity of the older Christian Socialists—Maurice, Kingsley, and Hughes—fired the enthusiasm of their disciples, and led them, now as teachers and now as co-operators, through personal intercourse to such a knowledge of working men, their character, their capacity, their aims and claims, as awakened a new sense of affinity with their manhood, and sympathy with their efforts after amelioration. The extension

of primary and the reform of secondary education made the more open-minded men of the older universities, see the intellectual promise and abilities of those who had hitherto been excluded from the higher culture. The finely blended speculative and practical genius of T. H. Green became a passion for the realization of the ideals of freedom and justice in all the grades of our social and in all the forms of our national life, and his personal influence imparted his passion to several generations of university men, who later expressed it in their own ways, now in economics, now in politics, and now in the church. The study of the industrial revolution in the spirit and through the philosophy of Green made Arnold Toynbee feel that the man who tended the machine must no longer be sacrificed to the machine he tended, but be made, even by the craft he followed, better as a man and more efficient as a citizen. The teachings of Carlyle distilled through Ruskin, and woven by him into the theories of art and the criticisms of life that were his message to the age, inspired with a will for service many who would otherwise have wasted their sensitive enthusiasm in admiration of dubious art. The Anglican revival, like the older evangelical, became in many of its sons a love of souls, and certain both of its priests and laymen made the East End of London the scene of as unselfish labours and as consecrated lives as the most heroic ages of the Church have known.

The result of these and similar causes is the

varied movements, outwardly so different, which have had as their common end help of the working classes, especially those whose lot is hardest and least hopeful. Hence have come Toynbee Hall with its sane and sagacious belief in the value of art for the squalid East End, and its brave endeavour to educate the universities by means of Whitechapel, and to save Whitechapel by the culture and service of the universities; Oxford House, with its intense conviction of the mission of the Church to the masses, though of a mission that the ordinary ecclesiastical agencies and methods are quite unable to fulfil; Mansfield House, with its strong, practical spirit, seeking to improve the houses, the amusements, the minds, the relationships, and the lives of the workers in the farther East End; the Wesleyan settlement at Bermondsey, with its noble religious zeal and broad philanthropy attempting at once to heal the bodies and save the souls of those it can reach; University Hall, with its intellectual energy and its belief in knowledge as a saving and civilizing power; and besides these a multitude of houses and missions independently and separately maintained by colleges and public schools.

But the first broad and most apparent result of these varied institutions is this, they have affected much more profoundly those who have conducted them than those for whose sakes they are being conducted. Men who, left to the ordinary tendencies of nurture and culture, would have seen things only through the eyes of the propertied and leisured classes, have come or are coming to study them through the eyes of those who eat their bread in the sweat of their brow, often finding but little bread for all their sweat and toil. And it has been found surely enough that the same things look wonderfully different when seen from those two opposite points of view. For largely out of these settlements, and the influences by which they have persuaded cultured minds to occupy, sympathetically, the standpoint of the labourer, there has come both an academic and a religious socialism, which is powerfully modifying political, economical, and ecclesiastical doctrine, and which promises to affect the teaching and practice of the churches as radically as it is affecting the spirit and the scope of our civil legislation. We are witnessing a process of conversion, but it is of the missionaries at the unconscious hands of those they were sent out to convert; and this is a process which may have the most momentous results for the future of society and religion in England.

2. But correspondent to the new feeling which these causes have been contributing to produce in the churches, is the birth of a new spirit in the lower labour. It is possessed of a hopefulness which may be described as the child of a new sense,—on the one side, of internal competence or capability, and on the other, of the sympathy which comes from being better understood. In other words, it does not feel so much in bondage to its own infirmities, or so much an outcast from the com-

munity of freedom and progress and hope. This has been illustrated by those recent events in our economic history, which showed, first, the ability of the classes that live by what is termed unskilled labour to conceive methods and to use means for their own amelioration, and even to combine in support of them; and secondly, the willingness of classes once hostile or indifferent to assume a kindlier and more intelligent attitude to the disputes of labour, and even the tendency to regard its questions as the concern not simply of economics, but of social ethics. This spirit of sympathy from without labour which has so cheered the upward impulse from within it, stands in notable contrast to the jealous and fretful criticism which hindered and harassed the earliest attempts of the skilled workmen at combination. Both of these are hopeful elements, for the men who can design a policy of social and industrial improvement and unite in its support, have become something more and better than day labourers; while the society that looks at an industrial question through living persons and in its effects upon them, and not simply through the abstract ideas of capital and labour, production and distribution, has translated the problem as to wealth into one as to well-being. The laws of political economy may be regarded in the one case, as in the other, as expressing actual processes or relations between co-ordinated phenomena, but they will be supplemented in the one case, as they would not be in the other, by the attempt to discover those countervailing forces, or to create those modifying conditions, that shall change their morally indifferent or sectionally injurious action into one socially and collectively beneficent. For economics may show the need of change, and the alternative lines along which it may move ; but it is the function of the social conscience to say which line the common good makes the more imperative. Thus economics may tell that *either* rent, *or* interest, *or* wages, must rise or fall, but it belongs to ethics to say which of these has the prior right to consideration in the adjustment of the upward or downward scale.

We may, then, venture to affirm that the ethical is the strongest and most significant tendency in social and political thought. And so men are coming to see more clearly that, for moral rather than economical reasons, questions between classes are never merely class questions, and that what depresses the standard of living in any one class lowers the level and worth of life throughout the community as a whole. And this idea is so penetrating the community that we see it daily becoming more distinctly conscious that it is as responsible for safeguarding the skill which is the sole property of the artisan, and, as far as possible, securing his happiness also, as for protecting his employer in the use and enjoyment of his capital. And this is a point which the industrial struggle through which we are even now passing with so much pain and shame, is only the more defining and emphasizing. In no previous economic struggle has the sense of justice within the community been so widely and deeply touched, or so vigorously expressed. The feeling has grown that both masters and men have a responsibility to the community as well as to each other, and that the community has such a responsibility to both as will not allow it to stand as an idle or uninterested spectator of the disastrous strife. The awakening sense of justice means that legislation embodying it will most surely follow, and this legislation will seek to deal justly with both classes—with the demand of the men for a living wage, and of the masters for guarded property and fair profits,—and will attempt to secure that each class shall deal justly by the other, and both by the community as a whole. It seems, then, as if we were tending towards a state where we shall have greater unity of feeling and solidarity of ethical interests ; and where these are, there will be more of the pressure of the community upon the class than of the dominion of the class over the community, though, it must be confessed, this is a state where wisdom and justice are demanded as they were never demanded or needed before.

3. Now, the most efficient factors of this change have been many, labour itself being the most efficient factor of all. Our workmen are no longer dumb ; we cannot now speak of them with Carlyle as the inarticulate multitude. They have a mind of their own and a most potent voice, while they have been

represented by many convinced and persuasive spokesmen. The economics of the school and the study do not now reign in undisputed supremacy; they are confronted and challenged by the economics of the workshop and the trades-union. And while we may here leave thesis and antithesis to qualify each other, we must confess that not only has the workman's experience forced the student to modify his doctrines, but his arguments have also conquered many of the prejudices and modified the mind of our English public, which, though often unreasonable and hard to convince, is invariably, when convinced, a mind both honest and just. Yet while the workmen themselves have been the most efficient factors of this changed attitude to their questions, we may say that those who have given the most remarkable and emphatic expression to the change have been churchmen, princes of the Roman, bishops of the Anglican, pastors of the Nonconformist communions. It is not said or meant that these were the men who formulated the principles or inaugurated the movements that effected the change,—this, we have just said, the workmen were and the churchmen certainly were not; but they expressed it, gave the sort of social sanction that made society aware of the process that was going forward, of the new feelings towards labour, its state and claims, that were rising within it. The really significant thing is that Roman priests, English bishops, and dissenting ministers have so tried to intervene, or have so succeeded in intervening, as arbiters between masters and workmen as to express the idea that conflicts between capital and labour concern as well the whole community, and especially the religious societies within it, as the immediate parties to the quarrel. They represent the pressure of the more reasonable social mind, or the more sensitive conscience, upon the belligerents. This is the most obvious moral to be drawn from the negotiations, whether successful or abortive, in connection with the strikes of the dockers in London, the shoemakers at Northampton, the miners in Durham, and with the locked-out at Hull. These events have not, indeed, the intrinsic significance of the fact we noticed above, the action of the working men on the strong and sensitive minds that have chosen to work for or live among them. Those events are significant as expressing common tendencies and achieved results, but this action as denoting nascent yet potent causes. The meaning of the former can in a manner be already measured, the latter is only a little bit of leaven just begun to act within the lump.

II

THE ATTITUDE OF THE MEN TO THE CHURCHES

1. But while the churches through their most honoured representatives, or through their strongest and most resolute sons, have turned this friendly and helpful face towards labour, what has been its cor-

respondent or reciprocal attitude? The help has been accepted with a sort of proud yet indulgent gratitude, as if for duty at last performed by one who had not been accustomed to perform it; but there has been little sign of any changed attitude to the faith and worship of the Church. The men who represent labour, and the labour they represent, may be quite willing to enlist the ecclesiastic as a recruit, but they show no inclination of joining the army he leads, or of submitting to his discipline. They may hail the attempt of the Church to fulfil economic functions, whether as mediator or as teacher, or even seriously propose to capture her as the chosen citadel of the capitalist, and turn her into the stronghold of labour and the minister of the democracy; but they do not mean to commit themselves to her, whether as regards her policy for this life or her dogmas as to the life to come. Nor need we wonder at their attitude; we are rather tempted to commend it as both reasonable and reverent. The Church is infinitely more than an economic institution; the man or society would be a secularist of the very worst type who would enter it simply because of its promise to be profitable for the life that now is. This is a reason worthy of the suitor for social recognition, but not of the blunt integrity of the English workman. Then all churches are historical institutions; the attitude to them of classes and bodies of men is also historical. Agreement on a current question does not affect an attitude which depends on ancient and permanent causes. If, then, we would discover how the Church and the industrial classes are to be reconciled, we must inquire into those causes which worked their estrangement and still keep them estranged. This estrangement is too general to be explained by any local or accidental or occasional cause, or indeed any cause that affects only one of the two sides. The causes are of so common and so essential a kind that they have affected and do affect equally the churches and the industrial classes, both in themselves and in their mutual relations.

2. It may be doubted whether the estrangement can properly be described as general; but it is general in this sense that (the Græco-Russian Church does not come into our purview) it is a state which all churches know and have cause to lament. The experience of the Roman Church is not uniform, but it is decisive enough. There is no country where the anti-clerical and anti-Church feeling is so strong as in France, and it is intensest—becoming almost a sort of fanaticism—in the artisan class. The Belgian workman is less demonstrative and more tolerant than his French neighbour, but quite as little does he love the Church. There is no Church in the United States that suffers so much from leakage, or the loss of those immigrants and their descendants who were hers by race, as the Roman Catholic. It is, of course, different in Ireland, in the South American Republics, and in certain of the countries of Southern Europe; but it is only different in these

cases because the industrial development has been arrested, or has not well begun. In the case of Ireland, indeed, there is this special characteristic: Catholicism and patriotism have only been different aspects of the same thing, church and people lay under the same disabilities, suffered from the same penal laws, and were therefore one in their conflict for justice and freedom. But as regards the general question the significant thing is, that where industry has been so far developed as to allow the causes which most tend to alienation to operate, the Roman religion has, so far from preventing, emphasized and exasperated the effect. The Anglican Church, too, has here failed signally, often in spite of her many beneficences, sometimes even because of the form her beneficences have assumed. There are districts in England where, if it had not been for certain dissenting bodies, paganism would have practically prevailed. Her debt to those bodies she can never pay, and, unhappily, she is not always willing even to recognize it, at least in a form that an honourable creditor can regard as recognition. Methodism, in its several branches, has done more for the conversion and reconciliation of certain of the industrial classes to religion than any other English Church. It is but just to say that the enfranchisement of our mining and agricultural populations made this evident, that their regulative ideas were religious rather than utilitarian and secular. The politician finds when he addresses the peasantry that he has to appeal to more distinctly ethical and religious principles than when he addresses the upper or middle classes, and we may hope that even in a politician the principles he appeals to may ultimately affect his policy. Meanwhile we simply note that it is the local preacher rather than the secularist lecturer who has, while converting the soul, really formed the mind of the miner and labourer, and who now so largely represents the ideas he seeks in his dim and inarticulate way to see applied to national policy and legislation. The Congregational and the Presbyterian Churches have been more successful with the middle than with either the lower or the upper classes ; they may indeed be said to represent the older English Nonconformity, but while the latter is largely Scotch, the former inherits the mind and traditions of the burghers and the yeomen who formed the main body of the Independents of the Commonwealth. Theirs were the men who governed England from '32 to '68, and who have not been inactive since then. They are mainly the men who have created our industries and extended our commerce, and made the conscience for integrity and economy in the English race. These things are not said by way of polemic against any church, or of apologetic on behalf of any ; but simply by way of stating a fact that needs to be explained. Of all forms of ecclesiastical controversy, the most sordid and mean is the form of mutual reproach, or blame for failure where there has been common guilt. The body that has helped to keep any class or any proportion of any class religious, deserves the gratitude of all the rest ; the body that has failed, though it has tried to succeed, deserves at least their sympathy and respect. But when our churches stand face to face with the alienated classes of our great cities and industries, the only mood that becomes any and is incumbent upon all, is one of humiliation and confession of sin with a view to amendment of life. But this only emphasizes our special point—where the effect is so general there must be common causes more or less uniform in their operation. Our problem is the discovery and the determination of these causes.

III

CAUSES, APPARENT AND REAL, OF ALIENATION

1. Now among these causes I do not reckon as primary, either in time or in importance, what is popularly known as infidelity or unbelief. No doubt there is among artisans under various forms and names a great deal of vigorous and thoroughgoing negation. Forty years ago it used to be termed Secularism, which was a sort of instinctive and unreasoned agnosticism. Its basis was a rough-and-ready doctrine of utility, which regarded this life as the only real object or field of knowledge, and judged everything by its value or efficiency in helping man to live it honestly and happily. Then, under the new scientific impulse, came a wave of more positive

materialism, and doctrines and dicta from men like Darwin and Huxley, down through Tyndall to Moleschott and Buchner, were repeated and interpreted into a sort of philosophy of existence, though now and then an ideal or intellectual element was so introduced as to modify the conception into a species of Pantheism. The criticism which was its polemic against Christianity, especially so far as directed against the Scriptures as sources or authorities in religion, was mainly antiquated, as it were a posthumous Deism. The remarkable thing is that the infidelity of the working man is essentially derivative, an acquired or borrowed thing; and the men from whom he has borrowed it were those of the eighteenth century, with their hard and prosaic spirit, their unhistorical sense, their inability to see anything in the historical records of the received religion, save the unreason or combined folly and hypocrisy of the present in professing to believe that such books could be of divine origin and authority. We may say, then, that this borrowed infidelity is an effect rather than a cause of the working man's estrangement from the churches; it is an apology for the attitude he holds, rather than the reason why he assumed the attitude. So far as careful inquiries and observation may be trusted, we may venture to affirm that the number of unbelievers to the whole class is proportionally small, though it contains some men of marked integrity and independence of mind. Since, then, the intellectual reasons or difficulties must be held to be secondary causes of disbelief, we may find the primary in a moral conviction, the belief that the churches are not religious realities, not bodies organized for the teaching and doing of righteousness, but for the maintenance of vested interests and conventional respectabilities. There is disbelief in the churches rather than in religion, though, when the disbelief becomes articulate, it tends to extend to the ideas and history involved in the claims and creeds of the churches.

The distinction between disbelief in religion and in the churches may seem illicit, but is, in fact, both radical and real. The one may be said to be intellectual, but the other social or moral and emotional in its origin ; the one comes to a man through education, but the other through the experiences of life. Disbelief in religion may be conjoined with conformity to a church ; disbelief in the churches involves the refusal to be identified with their religion, or to join in their profession and worship. The former is a state of things not unknown in the upper and educated classes ; the latter is more congenial to the franker and less illumined intellect of the workman. The cultured man lives in a world of delicate shades and fine gradations ; doubt may come through a hundred channels, till the strenuous faith of the past or the convinced present seems to him only a series of childlike illusions ; but he may so feel the inconvenience both for himself and others of disturbing the established order that he will prefer to act as if what he knew to be illusions he believed to be realities The workman, on the other hand, lives in a world of well-marked lines and clear-cut realities ; his thinking has always the merit of directness and simplicity, while his logic works with the rigour of his own machines, and so if he comes to the conclusion that certain things are illusory or unreal, he finds it most convenient to act in harmony with the conclusion to which he has come. Hence the man of culture may be a speculative agnostic or philosophic sceptic, or even in things critical and historical, a rationalist, but at the same time, for reasons that weigh with his conventional conscience, a conforming churchman and even an ecclesiastical conservative. But this attitude is simply unintelligible to the unsophisticated mind of the artisan, and so to assume it is impossible to him ; he simply cannot understand how it can be an honest thing to join in professions you have ceased to believe, or spare institutions whose central ideas you conceive to be imaginary or false. The two unbeliefs are thus generically unlike ; the one is the unbelief of a man whose mind has outgrown the faith of a world with whose social order he is satisfied, and wishes to maintain ; the other is the unbelief of a man who is dissatisfied with the social order in which he finds himself, and so comes to doubt the ideas which are invoked as its sanction and basis. The former infidelity is the child of the intellect, but the latter of experience ; the one cultivates a doubt which allows or even requires him to support the church, but the other faces a church which he so conceives as to be compelled to doubt. In the one position there is fatal insincerity, in the other vigorous veracity; and the church which knew its opportunity and mission would hope more from the mind that denied and opposed than from the mind that doubted and conformed.

2. We have been concerned here simply with the analysis of phenomena that are familiar to every one who knows and has observed both the educated and the working classes. And this analysis has illustrated the position that the infidelity of the latter is an effect rather than a cause of the alienation from the churches, while it helps to explain the derivative character of the arguments used to defend and maintain it. But this only throws us back on the prior question as to the causes of this alienation. And here two things have to be observed: first, these causes are not of yesterday, but are old, have been almost imperceptible in growth, and gradual yet continuous in· their action ; and secondly, they have not been incidental or occasional, but belong to the complex process which has produced our present social order. The function of the Church is not simply to maintain an established Christianity, but to create it anew in the spirit and conscience of each successive generation. We use very general, and, it may be, altogether misleading terms when we speak of the present as being the heir of the past. The heir, in order to possess, must recreate or reconstitute his

inheritance, assimilate it in form of being and mode of action to himself and his world. The remarkable thing in the law of heredity, whether individual or collective, is not what man does, but what he does *not*, inherit. The son may repeat his father's features, colour, voice, gait, and even his minuter tricks or niceties of manner, but yet be, as regards mind, character, faith, his exact opposite, *i.e.* he inherits the accidents or outward semblance, not the intrinsic qualities or distinctive characteristics. And this means that the new individual constitutes, in a perfectly real sense, out of himself and from among the old conditions a new world. And the same principle governs the evolution of society, though, as it works here on so vast a scale, the succession is less rapid, the changes more gradual, the contrasts not so violent. It is no mere fancy of the philosophical historian that each century has a character of its own; it is by what is distinctive in the character of each that the progress of the world is measured.

Now, it is in conformity with this law that we say that each generation must have a Christianity of its own born anew within it, and not simply repeating the traditions or appropriating the habits of the fathers. No single generation has ever been completely Christianized, and even the most Christian of all the past generations, whether primitive or mediæval, would, were it re-incorporated and judged by our more exacting modern standards, be considered hardly Christian at all. The simpler a society is, the simpler will its religion be ; the more complex the society, the richer in all its elements and the stronger in all its forces must the religion become, especially if it has to satisfy the whole nature, command and inspire the whole of life. Now, the social evolution has with us been vaster and more rapid than the religious or ecclesiastical. Society has changed as the Church has not ; it falsifies its living past by attempting to retain in a new world the organization, methods, ideals that were made in an old, and were excellently adapted to the world in which they were made, and to a vigorous life within it. Adaptation to environment is a necessity to all organisms ; it is only by variation of form that continuity of life can be secured. Where the Roman Church has been most successful in maintaining her ancient ascendency in the ancient form, she has either annihilated progress, *i.e.* stopped the evolution of a higher order in society, as in Spain, or she has helped to reduce it to a mediæval turbulence, as in the South American Republics. But in Protestant countries the social development has outrun the religious, and it will only be by the religious development overtaking the social that the Church will be able to reclaim the masses.

This, then, is the general position : the alienation of the industrial classes from the Church is a result of this process of uneven or unequal development, or of the successive stages by which the Church has lost adaptation to the environment within which it lives. But what this means will become evident only when we have considered the stages or forms of this process in detail.

IV

INFLUENCE OF THE POLITICAL DEVELOPMENT

We begin with the action of our modern political thought and history on the mind and feelings of the classes which here concern us. Of this immense subject only a few salient points can be touched.

1. At the outset two things must be noted—first political and religious thought are so organically related, that each is but a form of the other. Political thought is the religious idea applied to the State, and the conduct of its public affairs, while religious thought is but our view of the polity of the universe, and man's relation to it. It follows that as man thinks in the one field, he comes to think also in the other; the unconscious logic which develops our instincts or intuitions into judgments is often much more rigorous than the conscious reasoning which builds up our intellectual system of things. And it is by force of this unconscious logic that the classes who reason because they feel, bring their political and religious ideas into harmony. And secondly, we live in the first century since the foundation of the world in which these classes have

by a process of gradual and ordered change been, as it were, emancipated, become, even as those who were erst their superiors, possessed of political power. The promise of the first Christian preachers Christian states are only now beginning to try to fulfil; and though this result has been achieved through the action of Christian ideas, yet it has not seldom been in the face of the now active and now passive resistance of Christian societies, or their official representatives.

In the Middle Ages, the political and the ecclesiastical systems were strictly supplementary and harmonious; the one was feudal, the other papal, and both within their limits and after their kind patriarchal. The King was head of the State, and all within it held under him; the Pope was head of the Church, and all within it held under him. Each in his own order reigned by divine right, though attempts were made to limit the power of the one by charters and by parliaments, and the authority of the other by creeds and councils. But the qualifying force was lodged in the one case in the barons and burghers, in the other in the bishops and clergy; as regards both the multitude was dumb, made to be ruled and to obey, not to reason and advise. The civil and ecclesiastical potentates might reason and negotiate and differ concerning their respective authorities or provinces, but in these high affairs the people had no voice; they had to suffer the ban or the blessing, as the one or the other of the rival authorities decreed. The Saxon serf in some respects hardly differed from the

Roman slave, and though the English burgher and yeoman conquered his freedom, the peasant remained the son of the bondwoman, without a voice in the assembly of his people.

In consequence of the change of religion the old factors of order in England were new combined, the forces from beneath were not relieved and called into play. The King could without fear of the Pope affirm his divine right, and he so did it as to compel the barons and the burghers and the yeomen to qualify his rights by theirs. They, after a century of struggle, triumphed, and after the kings by divine right came a line which reigned by the grace of the aristocracy and gentry. The rights that now governed were those of property, and they proved even more merciless to the peasant and the workman than the feudal overlord or the autocratic king. They did not assert themselves by means of vassalage or villenage or arbitrary exactions, but mainly by the slow growth of claims which devoured ancient privileges, and of new laws which abolished old liberties and rights. And under this reign the people were helpless, almost as dumb as they had been in the old feudal days. But change was at hand; the idea of free speech penetrated downwards, and with it a new order of rights began to be conceived. There are writers who can cleverly demonstrate the logical absurdities that lie in such phrases as "the rights of man," and by analysis eliminate the idea of rights from any conception of him that can be formed. But all phrases are relative, and have some historical occasion which must be known if they are to be understood. " The rights of man" is a phrase which must be construed as the antithesis to the rights of special or favoured classes, kings or priests or peers. It denotes the idea which Knox expressed in his fine reply to Queen Mary: "And what are you in this commonwealth?" "A subject born within the same, Madam;" and because a subject with a place as real and rights as valid and claims to consideration as sacred as those of the sovereign. Once this idea had penetrated the mind of the multitude, the hour of deliverance from the narrower and more violent rights, regal, clerical, baronial, was at hand.

2. But the new ideas had to struggle hard first for a footing, then for victory; and the conflict was carried on not without sweat and dust. The established political and ecclesiastical order had been, as it were, woven in the loom of time into a single web, and to unweave the web seemed like undoing the chief work of time, dissolving society into chaos. On the one side, men defended the political order that they might save the ecclesiastical; on the other side, men assailed the ecclesiastical, which was the more vulnerable, that they might reach the political. The supreme calamity of French Catholicism, or rather the crime which no later sufferings can ever atone for, was its alliance with the king and the Court. The king had been a convenient instrument in the religious wars; by his help Protestantism

was practically annihilated, and it was thought that since he was so good for one thing, he could be made equally good for all. As his will was sovereign, to control him was to control France. And so the great concern of Catholicism was to keep possession of the king, which it did without being too curious as to the kind and quality of the king possessed. But in being so careful of him it lost the people, and put into the hands of his enemies, who were therefore also the enemies of his church, the most tremendous weapon that was ever levelled against religion. For in their fury the assailants did not distinguish religion from the men who betrayed it, and Christianity was made to bear and to suffer for the sins of Catholicism. And it did suffer. There never was a raillery like Voltaire's, a mockery so pitiless, so charged with scorn, so heated through and through with passion, yet so perfectly controlled and adapted to its end. While he incarnated, he did not exhaust the spirit of revolt ; he only inaugurated its reign. The Encyclopedists opposed the illumination to superstition ; Rousseau the state of nature to the state of custom and convention and fictitious inequality. And so the conflict spread from religion and the Catholicism which was held to be its only real and adequate embodiment, to society and the State. The denial passed through the church to the king it had crowned with divine rights and declared to be most Christian ; it was seen that he had neglected his duties to the lives, as much as the church had neglected its duty to the minds of men. And so the movement which began with the Christ of the Roman Church as "the Infamous" it was to erase, ended in the erasure of the monarch. The two that had stood together that they might abolish the Protestantism of the seventeenth century, fell together in the consequent revolution of the eighteenth.

3. But France largely determined the spirit and form of our modern political thought, and helped to give it, especially so far as the people are concerned, so much the character of a religious revolt. The books which had at the end of last century, and throughout the first half of this, by far the greatest influence on the awakening mind of the English artisan, *The Age of Reason* and *The Rights of Man*, were steeped in the spirit of France and the Revolution. No doubt they found here friendly conditions. The Established Church was torpid, and a guardian of obnoxious interests rather than a teacher of neglected duties. The middle classes were in the hands of the old dissent, the peasantry were being reached by the new Methodism; but for the artisan no one seemed specially to care. His food was a radical philosophy, a popularized version of the *Encyclopédie;* he lived in the age of reason, and believed in the charter and the rights of man. There is a remarkable difference at this period in the respective attitudes of the middle and the working classes to politics and religion. The middle classes were essentially religious, Tom Paine was a name they abhorred; but they were vigorous reformers, anxious to repeal

disabilities, to simplify and ameliorate law, to facilitate the creation and distribution of wealth, to husband the national resources, and to use them in the most economical, yet profitable and productive way. They had great respect for property, and no theory as to the abstract or innate rights of man as man which they thirsted to apply to politics in general, and the suffrage in particular. But the working classes were more rigorously philosophical; they were governed by ideals which they had reasoned out and applied to the organization of the State; a man, simply because he was a man, was sacred in their eyes, and possessed of rights which were proper to himself, and did not depend on any property, great or small, he might hold. On this ground they pleaded for political justice, and the changes it required were matters of right, not of mere expediency, which, indeed, was to them a peculiarly abhorrent conception. But to this political philosophy the Church was a greater offence than the State; it was the apotheosis of inequalities, loved rank and wealth, privilege and prescription, forgot the poverty of its founders, who had laboured with their hands, and of all the beatitudes most believed the one the Master had neglected to utter, *Beati possidentes.* With the Anglican Church, then, they felt that as now constituted they could have no part or lot. As Established it was the creation of privilege, as Episcopal it embodied to them the hated aristocratic principle, as administered, it regarded the people as children or paupers, and not as reasonable and independent men. As to the Free Churches, those of the older dissent were too plutocratic, too much governed by class feeling— an interested society, whose heart was where its interests were, with the employers and the tradesmen ; while those of the later dissent were too emotional, too little intellectual, so concerned with the future as to forget the present. So they reasoned, and they acted as they reasoned ; stood aloof from the churches, criticized them, disliked them, doubted their reality, denied their sincerity, and became sceptical of all they believed.

4. So far we have been strictly historical and expository, but now it is time to confess that the churches had in them more than enough to justify this attitude. Since then they have changed in many ways for the better, but they must be prepared to change still more if they would win back what they have lost. For one thing, it is impossible to maintain an aristocratic church in a democratic state, save, indeed, as the church of the aristocracy, their dependents and imitators. Such a church is easy to maintain, at least so long as the aristocracy are able and willing to maintain it ; yet its maintenance is, as regards national religion, a thing of infinite insignificance. We need the same sort of harmony between the ideas of Church and State in the modern as there was in the mediæval mind. Only in a feudal state can a papal church be in place, and a church which contradicts the whole spirit and genius of democracy may within a free state be the church

of a class, but can never be the home of the collective people. The principles that regulate their political will regulate their ecclesiastical thinking; in a State "broad based upon the people's will," the only church that has any chance of continuance must be one whose polity has the same basis, and the will that is the basis must be the main factor of order and organization. Of course, a church may argue that its polity was a matter of revelation, that its order was given to it, that its orders have been historically maintained, and are of its very essence. But these are to the people mere theories; about them scholars may like to argue—for they are persons who dearly love discussions about points where conjecture has free scope and positive proof is impossible; but for men of thought or action such theories have no worth. Yet, however this may be, one thing is clear, the will that has become an efficient factor in the State will never be content with a Church which simply reduces it into a mere receptivity or political inefficient. And the people are even more within their rights in claiming an active place in the conduct and legislation of the Church than in those of the State. They are but returning to the original idea and practice. The early churches were real democracies; their citizens had all the privileges of the fully enfranchised; and the constituents of the modern ought to have the place and the privileges of those of the ancient churches. But, of course, the cardinal principle of the ancient Church must be maintained in the modern;

its people must be the people of God, for what other sheep can be of this fold? On this matter the democratic feeling is altogether sound; it loves reality, dislikes sham, pretence, and make-believe. It does not wish to see a man who has no religion busy himself with religious concerns; it does wish to see a man who professes religion be and do as he professes. And if the Church be organized and administered by the really religious, and look jealously to the character of those who compose it, then certainly the English workman will be the first to give it the homage of that respect which is the earliest and simplest form of faith.

V

INFLUENCE OF SOCIETY AND THE SOCIAL SPIRIT

1. But there are social tendencies and a social temper which are even more divisive in their action than political thought and feeling. These seem to be increasing in strength rather than decreasing. The more highly specialized our industrial life becomes, the more divided our society appears to grow. The plutocracy is ever pressing on the heels of the aristocracy, and with the small pride but great vanity that seeks to forget the rock whence it was hewn, it deepens, in the very degree that it succeeds, the line that divides the upper from the lower classes. Masters and workmen are every year growing farther apart, becoming rivals that with fear and distrust jealously

watch and willingly outwit each other. The old personal relations between them are being lost. Limited liability companies are employers, but not masters, and directors feel responsibility to shareholders a more immediate and exacting thing than concern for their men. Associations and unions, too, tend to place their relations on a strictly impersonal and financial basis. The master will not act without the approval of his association, or the workman without the sanction of his union, and they negotiate through officials and in pursuance of a policy rather than as men. Then the new social hunger affects both. The unions differentiate the workmen. The skilled and unskilled are divided by a gulf over which intelligence of each other's wellbeing can hardly pass. The finest gradations of feeling and social sense distinguish the various crafts, and within what seems the same craft status is determined by the quality and rarity of the skill. And why should not an aristocracy of art be known to workmen as well as to artists ? why may social distinction, based on the kind and degree of skill required, be allowed to professions and denied to handicrafts ? Still, if the unions differentiate the craftsmen they unite the workers, but the social joins with the industrial tendency in making the division from the employer absolute. The master does not love to live among his men ; he prefers the society of his suburb ; most of all, where he can command it, a town house where he and his womankind can see society and enjoy the gaieties of the season. This is a feature ominous of serious social change. The old Lancashire and Yorkshire manufacturer was a man of shrewd mind, but simple tastes. He lived quite plainly, and he worked hard. And though he and his work-people had many a tussle, ending now and then in a violence and destruction quite unknown in these days, yet they knew each other, understood each other, and learned through their common life and toil to cultivate a sort of genial brotherhood. But the head of a great firm is mostly invisible; he is a name to his people, and nothing more; his people are to him part of his machinery, distinguished from the other parts by being less manageable, and when deranged more difficult to repair. And so they tend to fall ever farther apart, to influence each other less, to be less just to each other, to care for nothing save the profit to be got from the labour the one seeks to sell and the other to buy.

2. Now the churches have hitherto tended to follow the path of increasing social specialization, which is the line of least resistance, and to grow into societies for the demarcation and consecration of class. And the more they have done so, the more distasteful they have become to working men. There is nothing they so abhor as the social distinction which claims a religious sanction and assumes a religious shape; it wounds them in the most sensitive part. They cannot believe in a God who regards a man as any the better for the accident of

his birth, or of superior dignity because of his rank, and they will not respect a society which claims to represent God on the earth, and yet puts its trust in the House of Lords, or boasts of its aristocratic connections, or leans for support on some plutocrat who is loudly generous without being plainly just. Nor are they any more enamoured of churches composed altogether of people of their own class, for this is only another sort of insult to their sensitive pride. And this pride expresses a true feeling, the feeling that as all men are equal before God, so in His church there ought to be no respect of persons,—saintliness alone being recognized as honourable and distinguished. And this feeling may be, and ought to be, as much outraged by the workman who will not for social reasons worship with his master, as by the master who will not for similar reasons worship with his workman. If wealth were wise, there is nothing it would more dread than the separation of classes in the house of God, or the separation of different houses of God to different classes; and if it were good as well as wise there is nothing it would so little allow. The master who goes to worship where only other masters are, does his best to alienate himself from his people, to lower religion in their eyes, and to bring on the social revolution; for the only salt that can preserve society is sympathy and communion in the most serious things of the spirit between all classes. And this means that into the Church the sense and the air of social superiority must not be allowed to come. The attitude of patronage or condescension is here entirely out of place and purely mischievous; for in matters of religion the cottage may be more able to play the Lady Bountiful to the hall, than the hall to the cottage. And the Church, if it is wise, will prefer a workman qualified to serve to even a qualified master; for while society is always ready to honour position, it ought to be the distinction and privilege of the Church jealously both to see and to show that it honours spiritual fitness, and not rank or social status. And if master and workman are associated on equal terms in Church affairs, they will attain the mutual knowledge and develop the mutual respect that will make intercourse on other things more pleasant and reasonable. If the Church could secure this service according to spiritual gifts, it would do more for social order and stability than any possible legislation.

This is written in a Scotch manse, and under the influence of the memories it awakens. Here presbytery has been an extraordinary power; of the religious people of Scotland ninety *per cent.* are within its fold, and its power has been largely due to its parity, the way in which it has enlisted men of all classes in the service of the Church. It was within my recollection no unusual thing to see as members of the same session, all duly ordained elders charged with the spiritual oversight of the congregation, the laird, the schoolmaster, the doctor, the farmer, the farm servant, or shepherd; and of these I have known the last to be the man of finest character, of most wisdom in council and greatest spiritual weight in the congregation or parish. Indeed, as a fact, from the experience of one who was himself for several happy years the moderator of a kirk-session, this ought to be told—that the person who above all others stands out in his memory as a man of delicate feeling, of clear, yet charitable judgment, was a working quarryman. And the presence of such a man in a high ministerial office, elected and ordained to it by the act and sanction of the Church, was a good to all concerned. The laird, the schoolmaster, the doctor, and the farmer could not but respect the hind or the shepherd whose words were often wiser than their own, and in him they respected his whole class. It, too, was dignified by the office he filled so worthily, and the words of reproof he had to speak at the cottage hearth, or of consolation at some humble death-bed, were tempered by a feeling of kinship, even when the sense of spiritual vocation most burdened his spirit. Again must I express the sober and deep conviction—the church that dares to associate its poor with its rich in the same service when both are alike qualified for it, is the only church entitled to command, or worthy to receive the obedience and the love of both.

VI

INFLUENCE OF THE INDUSTRIAL DEVELOPMENT

1. But beside the political and social tendencies we must place the industrial. The harder the struggle

for existence grows, the harder does it become to be religious. If the wolf is not only at the door, but has to be held out by sheer strength of muscle, we can scarcely expect the man who holds it to think of other, even though they be higher things. In order to worship there must be not only a day of rest for the man, but a rested man for the day. If its hours are mostly needed to sleep off the fatigue or lassitude of the week, it can be little used for worship. And if the only religious exercise of the week be on the Sunday, the exercise will soon grow burdensome and irritating. Now the conditions under which work is done are increasingly unfavourable to the cultivation of the religious spirit. Competition grows every year keener, the weaker men are pushed downward, the abler men find it harder to rise, or even to make a beginning, and where time is so imperious in its claims, little thought can be spared for eternity. Possibly the matter may be put most closely by the statement of an actual but most typical case—that of a Yorkshire village, which would be a goodly western town. It was once a great evangelical centre, had quite an army of home missionaries, and created congregations and schools in towns much more important but less religious than itself. Its industry was weaving, which it cultivated with old-fashioned leisure. The men wove in their own houses or sheds, regulated their own hours, and were never too busy to discuss a question in politics or a problem in theology. They had time after breakfast for morning prayers, and in the evening the family assembled for worship. It was the proud boast of the village that at least once every day the sound of psalm and of prayer could be heard in its houses. But steam came, and the power-loom and the great factory, with "Hands" whose hours and work were as rigorously regulated as the looms they tended. The old leisure, with the old home life it allowed, was no more. Breakfast became a hurried meal, time enough to eat, but time for nothing more; the men and women who came home in the evening were tired, so exhausted with the heated atmosphere that they craved the open air, with a sound in the ears that made the old animated talk an irritation. So the old habits were broken off, and new and less excellent habits formed. The women in the mill lost their domestic feeling, and became noisier, coarser, more masculine, liking the factory as freedom, hating the home as drudgery. And the men lost their old quieter and more intellectual interests, grew fond of excitement, of amusements noisier than the noisy looms. And so the passion was awakened for the athletics that supplied opportunities to drink and gamble, and the more it developed the more averse they became to the old religious life, indeed incompetent for it in its old staid simplicity. May we not say, then, that this industrial development has created conditions that have made religion indefinitely harder to the man who must keep pace with it in order to live?

2. But it is easier to see these evils than to discover

a remedy which the churches can supply. The evils are consequents inseparable from the conditions under which our industries have been developed, rather than from the development itself, and the remedy must come, not from arresting the development, but changing the conditions. Whatever makes the struggle for life not less strenuous or inevitable, but less mechanical and monotonous, will conduce to a happier spirit in the workman. It is not the work that kills idealism, but the sordid conditions within and without the worker. And of these the inner are the fontal; and so the first thing to be done is to enrich and ennoble his soul, beget in him purer tastes, and evoke higher capacities. This is a thing that ought to be considered from the very beginning of his intelligent being, attempted in our schools, and incorporated in our systems of education. The school ought to be made as bright and beautiful as possible, the imagination ought to be cultivated as well as the understanding, and artistic faculty made as real an end as technical skill. If taste or the intellect could be so developed that to satisfy it became as instinctive and imperious a need in the workman as in the cultivated lawyer, or doctor, or statesman,— and these are certainly often more cruelly overworked than he—then he would even as they pluck from the very heart of his toil the moments needed for the refreshment of his mind or the culture of his spirit. Then, there ought to be accessible to him places where he could cultivate the tastes which had been developed within. The bath has been a great refining agency, for physical is near of kin to spiritual cleanliness; but these both can flourish only where the means for their being can be found, and the churches ought to be as jealous about the conditions necessary to intellectual and spiritual health as our public authorities are about those needful for the physical. Museums, picture galleries, and palaces of delight may, without a prepared people, be worse than useless; indeed, only haunts for the idle; but to a people prepared they may be made high means of grace.

These two things, then, the churches ought to do their best to create and to cultivate, the faculties that need intellectual and spiritual exercise for their very being, and the opportunities and means for keeping them in exercise. For the more these become necessaries to a man, the more open will he be to religious and moral influences. But these things must not stand alone; recreation and amusement are growing necessities to our industrial population, and there are no agencies more able to refine or brutalize. And for the moment the brutalizing force seems the stronger. Gambling threatens to be the ruin of all manly sport, while the passions it evokes and the drinking it encourages are making great matches more a terror to decency than a recreation to weariness. To refine our amusements would be a most religious work, and one that religious societies might very well undertake, even with some hope of success.

Yet they would need to begin above rather than below; it is precisely in the point of amusements that the upper classes act most mischievously on the lower, and provoke the imitation that is here worst flattery. If the church could persuade our gilded youth so to improve their pleasures as to reform their manners, it would help to make the amusements of all classes purer and healthier. But the most needful thing of all is the recreation of the home, for in industrial England it has almost ceased to be. Increased domesticity means the increase of all the finer affections, the rise of all the more gracious cares, and hopes, and loves. And where these are, religion is never far away; and where they are not, it will only be an external and, as it were, manufactured thing. It seems, therefore, as if the recovery of the home were the final necessity of the situation. If only the Church could rebuild the home, it would create the conditions that would, even in the face of our modern industrial development, make all the old chivalries and graces of religion still possible.

VII

INFLUENCE OF THE INTELLECTUAL MOVEMENT

1. But alongside the industrial development we must place the intellectual. The last half-century has been a period of remarkable mental activity and change—certainly much greater among the working than among the leisured and professional classes.

In this period the penny morning and the halfpenny evening newspaper have been created, and has ceased to be a mere news-sheet or political organ, and become a medium for all sorts of intelligence—sporting and scientific, social and literary. The newspaper has become, as it were, a circulating national library containing all kinds of stuff, good, bad, and indifferent, always appetizing, though not always wholesome and refreshing. In the old Chartist days newspapers were few, but they were filled with a serious purpose, serious men read them, passed them from hand to hand, and seriously discussed their contents. Now, though many journals are high-toned, not a few are edited on the principle that they must please to live, and the pleasure they conceive is of no noble or generous order. There are society papers for the working as for the upper classes, and each is spiced with the sauce its readers most relish. Sensations are loved below as well as above, but their flavour depends not on mystery or innuendo, but on blunt brutality. The records of the police courts are racy reading, but still racier the filthy gossip of backstairs and sporting-house and club. The sins of the west end are well known in the east, the achievements of every noble lord who has distinguished himself in the divorce court or a gambling hell are written out in full; and where the follies and crimes of the aristocracy are concerned the democracy has a good memory. These things are read by many because unclean, but by others because they speak of judgment to come. And this element has a subtle way of penetrating even the graver thought and argument of the people. I shall never forget the loathing which was awakened by the gruesome and sensual suggestions, touching certain sacred persons and histories, made by what professed to be an organ of advanced thought. It was the severest shock my faith in the intellectual character of the freethinking workman ever received. But it was significant of the mental atmosphere created by the society newspaper wherever it circulates, whether among the upper ten thousand or the lower twenty millions.

Yet this is a digression on intellectual deterioration rather than development. Let us hope that these things represent only a muddy eddy in the main onward moving and clarifying stream; and then mark the signs of mental expansion and activity. The industrial classes have proved themselves to possess political capacity in a high degree. They have had statesmen and legislators of their own raising; their unions have exhibited as much organizing and administrative genius as could be found in any modern government. They are indeed, whatever view we may take of their means and action, a marvellous creation, accomplished in spite of innumerable difficulties, both internal and external. And this capacity is beginning to concern itself with the State. The old Chartist was primarily a politician ; he was concerned about legislation and government, he wanted to be a citizen and to have the State so constituted that there would be room and a function in it for him ; but the modern trades-unionist is primarily an economist, concerned about labour and its rights— how to sell it to the best advantage, and how to maintain its price even in a falling market. Yet, as the Chartist saw lying behind his politics the field of economics, so the Unionist looks through his economics at politics, not, indeed, as an end, but as a means : in other words, he comes to parliament through the union, and all legislation is but a vehicle for its economical action. But what concerns us here is the mental and moral discipline involved in the organization and administration of the unions, and so the kind and quality of the men now being formed within labour, both for its sectional direction and its place in national politics. They are within their own order distinctly statesmen and legislators, and their class must be measured by its highest and strongest members, not by its lowest and feeblest.

Then, education has extended, and still extends and improves ; the school is now common, and the School Board is a body with higher aims than the statesmen who created it ever dreamed of. The people are not so easily satisfied as their representatives, they want higher and more efficient instruction, and the more they control the board the more they get what they want. And so to the primary has been added the higher Board school, and to both the technical and the continuation school. And as the ability to read is created, so is the opportunity for its exercise. Free libraries and reading-rooms now exist in all our cities and considerable towns, their number still increases, and as fast as it increases the space is occupied and the demand rises for more. And there, through novel and history, through science and biography, through philosophy and theology, through criticism and poetry, the people are being educated, and by their own will and at their own expense are carrying forward the work of the schools. And a special literature is growing up to meet their demand. For their enlightenment science ceases to be technical, and becomes so simple that he who reads may run, history is cultivated by masters of literary style, travels are made as fascinating as fiction, and fiction is as full of accurate knowledge as if it were science. Men who once knew no story but the *Pilgrim's Progress* now read Thackeray and Dickens, Walter Scott and George Eliot ; or those whose only history book was the Old Testament, now read Carlyle and Froude, Gardiner and Lecky ; or those whose only poetry was Watts' or Wesley's Hymns, now study Tennyson and Browning, Arthur Hugh Clough and Matthew Arnold. And they cannot read these things without getting a certain largeness of view or a critical attitude that makes them impatient with everything that savours of a narrower and more unreasoning world.

2. Now, has there been any correspondent change in what passes for religious education? On the contrary, may we not say it stands where it did fifty years ago? Anything more fatuous than the policy of the religious communities on this matter it is hardly possible to conceive. They have been contented with their old standards, their old methods, their old agents. It is humiliating to think that the thing which the majority in the London School Board so fanatically fights for, is called religious education. The thing wanted is not to be got at the ordinary Board school or from the average Sunday School teacher; the churches must give it, make it their constant charge, do it as their most vital work, devote to it their finest and best equipped spirits. What is called religious education is, to speak the blunt truth, often only a preparation for scepticism. It is appalling to think what would happen were the highest mysteries of the Christian faith made into subjects and standards for the ordinary Board school; even in the hands of a skilful and reverent teacher they would appear as a series of antinomies that grew ever more incredible and ever less capable of reconciliation. These are things that only the most highly trained scholarly and philosophical intellect is qualified to teach, especially to boys. We can already see how the method has operated, and with what fatal results, in a region far less open to abuse than the doctrinal. Crude views of Biblical history crudely presented to a boy of four-

teen, and then confusedly remembered by him when he has become a man, may be said to be the material for the ideas as to religion and the Bible which are discussed and destroyed by the sulphureous criticism of the secular hall and the free-thinking press. The answer to their infidelity is not argument but education, yet education of the church that gives it, as well as of the men to whom it is given. It must be conducted in the school, but also in the home; must begin when the boy is a child, and not cease at the very moment when it is most needed, just as he is blossoming into the man, going out into the world and learning the gravity of work and the impotence of will. Yet in order to this the Church ought to be the school, for, to look at the matter under only a single aspect, the boy's relation to the school ends, and with it his education ceases, but his relation to the Church ought to be continuous, and its care for him a thing as constant and progressive as its responsibility. And here the most courageous is also the wisest policy; religious knowledge in the school is fixed and formulated, but in the Church is living and growing, and so the two give things generically different. The school may drill, but the Church communicates life. And simply because it deals with living knowledge, it cannot be held in bondage to standards and rigid formulæ. And here it is of cardinal moment that the wider thought should not be held back from the youth till he hears of it in the debating club or hall of science.

He ought to be taken as far into the confidence of the scholar and the mind of the religious thinker as he is able to go; and as the mind grows, instruction ought also to grow with the mind. And so far from being limited to the texts and the catechetical formulæ that are the hope of our Philistine School Board legislators, it ought to be made as many-sided and comprehensive as religion itself, sympathetic to poetry, akin to art, related to history, bound up with philosophy, embedded in science. If religion could only be so taught, then the whole education of our people would become a discipline in the knowledge whose end is piety and whose inspiration is God.

VIII

THE CONCILIATION OF THE ALIENATED

Our argument, so far as it has proceeded, may be stated thus: The present state of the working classes may be described as one of alienation rather from the churches than from religion; but this alienation has been due not to one but to many causes, which, as springing out of our whole modern development, have affected equally and radically both sides. The churches have of late manifested a changed feeling, are possessed of a new sense of their duty to end the alienation, but to this there is no reciprocal or correspondent feeling on the part of the working classes. As the estrangement has been gradual, the reconciliation must be the same, and it can only be accomplished by the Church as a whole reaching, and either neutralizing or removing all the causes of the alienation. This may involve large modifications in the polities and methods, and an enlargement in all the activities of our varied religious societies, but the Church cannot hope for exemption from the inexorable law that the organism that would survive in the struggle for existence must adapt itself to its environment. Grant these positions, and the problem follows : How is the Church not only to reach and remove the causes of alienation, but to reach and reconcile the alienated?

1. Now, it is evident, the Church can do this only as an essential part of the mission with which it has been charged—the saving of man. Its strength does not lie in policies or economic stratagems, in ceremonial pomp or impressive spectacles ; but in the truth it teaches, the life it communicates, and the character it forms. It may constitute a happy world out of good and happy persons, but it could never create an ordered society out of the most felicitous speculations, political, economical, or theological.

The first thing, then, for the Church to be is to be faithful to its own mission and ideal, to live and think and act as if it were indeed the Saviour of men. It exists, like its Founder and Head, not to be ministered unto, but to minister, and to give its life a ransom for the many. It ought to know neither aristocracy nor democracy, but only man ; its concern is neither with capital nor labour, but with the men who hold the capital or do the labour. Its work is to save souls, to teach truth, to enforce duty and discipline, in a word, so to cause the kingdom of God to come, that His will may be done on earth as in heaven. But this is the most radical work possible; it is deeper than politics, for it deals with the men who make and administer and obey the laws; it is more fundamental than economics, for it touches the sources and ends of wealth, the men who create and distribute, and who accumulate and apply it; it is more determinative than society, for it judges the social units, limits yet guards their rights, and tries their conventions. But the faithfulness must be to the whole mission. It is not enough for the Church to conceive itself as an institute for worship or preaching or the observance of ritual, or as a society adorned by official dignities and constituted by the orders that govern; it is necessary that it be transmuted by the fire of a great enthusiasm into the regenerator and moral guide of life. It must conceive itself as through and through ethical, as it were the embodied conscience and law of God, created expressly for the moral direction and inspiration or man. It ought to contend for purity of belief in order to purity of character, and to hold sin the one heresy that makes a man excommunicate. It must not mistake conformity to custom for obedience to moral law, or be so false in its standards as to allow a bad man to be a patron of its clergy or of their livings, while denying to a good man who serves Christ in his own way the name of Christian. Nor must it wink at sin in high places or in low, or allow its discipline to become a dead letter. And discipline is worse than a dead letter when it is so misguided as to condemn in a peasant what it fails to see in a peer, however flagrantly flaunted before its eyes, or when it spares the mystery of iniquity lying at its own door while angrily reproachful where the door chances to be a neighbour's. Discipline would be a tremendous power were it vigorously and righteously exercised ; where the law could not reach it would penetrate, the manifest sin that is more mischievous than open crime it would punish, and its penalties would follow the immoralities whose guilt is real, though, perhaps, not legal. And not till the Church be fearless in its discipline will it seem honest to those outside it ; but were it to prove its faith by enforcing its discipline, it would reclaim the masses by compelling them into admiration and belief.

The Church, then, will be strong only as it is just, and it will be just as it deals with men as men, and not simply as grouped into classes. It is as impossible to draw up an indictment against a class as against a whole people, and where an indictment cannot be drawn, a sentence cannot be passed. But the ambition of the Church will be to create men with a passion for righteousness, and to use all its forces and all its influences to have righteousness realized by every person in every class and in every region of our private and social, our industrial, commercial, and national life. It ought to be as incapable of servitude to a majority as to a monarchy, to the masses as to the classes, and it is certain that subservience is the surest way to forfeit both obedience and respect. And only as it is above suspicion will it be able to accomplish the work of reconciliation, and the more it can reconcile to itself the more will it create a happy and harmonious people. For the Church more than any other agency in our midst can play the part of mediator. Not by intervening in strikes and strifes, but by bringing about the understanding that will prevent their occurrence. The gospel came to make peace on earth by creating in men good-will, and there is no cause of ill-will like the conflict of interests conducted in the darkness of mutual ignorance and distrust. We are just being made to feel that the wars of industry may be as calamitous as the wars of peoples ; indeed, the strike or the lock-out is but civil war waged under the forms suitable to these days. Now, the Church should in the very process of fulfilling her duty do two things, first, teach men of all classes to be in the highest Christian sense religious men in all their offices, trades, and relations ; and, secondly, bring men of all classes together as men, make them to know each other, and look each at his own questions with the other's eyes. Men united and humbled before God, and inspired by a common sense of duty, might disagree, but the more they understood the more would they respect each other, and would the more reluctantly differ.

The workman needs to know the master that he may comprehend his case; the master needs to know the workman that he may understand where the shoe pinches, and how it can be made to fit the foot. If they could so meet together that the master would have to cease to think of the workman as a servant, or as a being of inferior nature with inferior rights to his own, and the workman would learn to think of the master as a man beset on all sides with responsibilities and the servant, or even victim, of forces he deeply dislikes, they would soon discover through their common natures the community of their interests and the duty, which they must somehow find a way to fulfil, of living together in peace. And the only agency by which they can be thus united and made mutually intelligible is a church which knows them as men, but refuses to know them as interests or as classes.

2. But over and above this general principle of fidelity to its own idea or mission, the Church must follow special lines or methods of action, and these ought to be as varied as the needs and minds of the people it would reclaim.

(1) The Church must appeal to the alienated mind, seek to persuade it by reason and argument. It must become in a larger degree the instructor of the people. In order to this it must think more and better of its own mission, of the truth it carries that it may interpret and realize. Here almost everything has to be done; we need to escape from the bondage of the letter into the freedom of the spirit.

The Church must be a learner before it can be a teacher, and it will find, when it speaks out of its own honest and living convictions, that none will hear more gladly than our workmen. Any man who has preached knows what a keen and appreciative audience they can form, more greedy of instruction than any upper or higher middle class congregation. It is in these latter that the impatience of the sermon has become decisive and uncontrolled, and this impatience largely means that instruction is not wanted because religion is conceived as a form or a service, not as duty and truth. Yet this cause does not stand alone. Nothing falls into contempt quite undeserved. Sermons worthy of respect will continue to be respected even by those who now conceive them as having no place in the worship of God. But the very desire for knowledge and direction makes the want or the inefficiency of the sermon a thing intolerable to the thoughtful working man. To meet his needs it must change its character and enlarge its range, must not fear to deal with the central questions of religion, to re-state and re-discuss the highest mysteries of Christianity, to handle the criticism and theology of the Scriptures, to reason concerning Christian ethics, and apply them to all the problems and occasions of life. There is nothing the pulpit so much needs as courage, both in its mode of handling things and in its choice of the things it handles; there ought to be nothing too high or too abstruse, too critical or too philosophical for it, any more than too plain or too practical. It may be that want of courage is only another term for want of capacity ; but whichever name be applied to the defect, it is one that every energy should be strained to repair and remove. The potentialities of the pulpit are incalculable ; hardly any limit could be set to what it might accomplish. The whole realm of thought and feeling, truth and duty, history and life, art and literature, knowledge and action lies before it ; crowds of anxious, expectant, perplexed, thoughtful men and women wait for its words. The mysteries that most appeal to the imagination, the history that most moves the heart, the hopes that most uplift, the fears that most abase, the motives that persuade the will, and the ideals that control the conscience are at its command, ready to be used as means to its ends and instruments of its power. What it needs is men ; if the Church could find men equal to its opportunity it would possess and govern the mind of England, possibly most of all the minds of its working men.

(2) The alienated life must be touched and changed. Carlyle long ago preached this gospel: " Soul is kindled only by soul. To 'teach' religion, the first thing needful, and also the last and the only thing, is the finding of a man who *has* religion." And what is the Church but a nursery for the making of such men ? But once they are made they must be distributed, the living soul must come face to face with the soul it has to quicken. And here much may be expected from colonies of the brave and good

in our East Ends, and in all the districts, urban, suburban, and rural, where our workers congregate; but hitherto these have been composed mainly of young men, and we must, by ceaseless help and replenishment, take care that their surroundings do not prove stronger than they. There is no civilizing or Christianizing power like that of a good person, and the good person is most needed where the good are few. A thoughtful and observant medical officer once said to me, "A single cleanly family raises the standard of cleanliness in a whole tenement, and I have seen the removal of one attended by deterioration all round." And what is true of outward is true of inward cleanliness. The presence of the morally healthy acts as a kind of moral deodorizer, and his absence is the despair of the worker in the slums. If, then, the moral and religious colony is to accomplish anything, it must be carried out on a vaster scale than has yet been dreamed of. The churches must not fear to give of their noblest and their best, who certainly will not themselves refuse to be given, to the service of the brothers who live by labour.

(3) But the place that most needs our care is the home where the alienated life is nursed and formed. We speak of the working man, and we forget his wife; but his wife is a more potent factor in his improvement or deterioration than he is himself. She suffers more in the struggle for life than he does, has fewer elements of change and brightness in her life, and readily falls into a hopeless drudge, unable

to cheer, because incapable of cheerfulness. Yet she is more susceptible of cheer from her sister woman than her husband from his brother man. Here is a field where splendid work may be done. The poor have had more than enough of parochial charities, and congregational visitors, and officious distributors of tracts which are seldom read. What they need is an army of good motherly or sisterly women, who will never be prying or condescending, but only patient and neighbourly, and who will stay in and cook the husband's dinner, or tend a fractious child, or even tidy up the room while the mother escapes from the hated four walls to breathe a fresher air and see a larger world. If we could only create the happier and more wholesome home, the battle were as good as won.

IX

URGENCY OF THE NEED

1. What we have called the reconciliation of the working classes is a matter of vital necessity both to themselves, the State, and the Churches. We live in the generation that has witnessed the transit of power, and this means that for the battle to maintain our place and fulfil our function in the history of humanity we have called out our last reserves. The evils of no past sovereignty were irremediable, for behind the reigning house or class we had reserves vaster than the army in the field. When the king was supreme, we had an aristocracy

often able, and always willing, to correct his blunders and save us from the results. When the aristocracy governed, we had the middle class, watchful, expectant, capable, eager to embody in legislation their larger and more noble conception of the State. When the middle class had exhausted their energies and realized their ideals, we had the people waiting the opportunity for the exercise of their still untried strength. And now their opportunity is come, our last reserves are summoned to the front, and on their skill and endurance the issue of the battle will depend. The moment is critical, for, as all history testifies, it is more easy to gain power than to exercise it wisely ; and our modern democracies are, for reasons partially stated in Lecture IV., the very converse of the ancient. The ancient democracies were all in a sense aristocracies, *i e.* they represented the reign of a dominant order or race. The demos might be coextensive with the citizens, but the citizens were not coextensive with the population, citizenship being rigorously limited to men of a given birth and blood. Then, too, the old democracies were municipalities rather than nationalities, their area was so limited, their politics so simple, their opportunities of discussion so multitudinous, their legislative machinery so potent and direct, that it was not difficult for the citizen to master the mysteries and the method of state-craft. He was trained in the discussion of political ideas from his boyhood ; the city which was his state lived before his eyes, its statesmen passed him daily on the street ;

his public life was but private life enlarged, and as he knew himself only through his family, so he conceived his family as only through and for the State. But our modern democracies are an almost complete contrast to this, especially in those things that concern the exercise of sovereign power. The causes, represented by the growth and reign of Christian ideas, which abolished slavery and serfdom, have made the modern demos coextensive with the manhood of the State. While the State is not a city or a confederacy of cities, but a series of nationalities, the people, into whose hands power has passed are not a select and homogeneous race, or the citizens of a small city welded together by pride of blood, local ambitions and jealousies, and the need of holding down a multitude of helots whose labour is necessary to their very being; but they are a mixed and heterogeneous multitude, as it were the helots rather than the citizens, not gathered into a single centre, but distributed through many provinces, each with a centre of its own, often more conscious of the many conflicting interests which divide them than of the few great common interests which unite.

Now, it is impossible to conceive anything more critical than the recognized and conscious sovereignty of a people so constituted and so placed, one more capable of infinite good or incalculable ill. And the earliest moments in the use of power must always be the most critical, for they are the formative moments. In the modern as in the ancient world there will be opportunity enough for a Cleon to attempt to lead by flattering the vanity or the foibles or the greed of the many; or for an Aristophanes to attempt by savage satire of Cleon or brutal caricature of Socrates to befool the many and secure power to the few. But, happily, there is always a limit to the influence of the demagogue, whether he be an avowed man of the people or a disguised oligarch, and the limit is soon reached and rarely transcended. The more real danger lies in the tendencies common to human nature, especially the tendency to use power to gratify narrow interests, or sectional passions, or immediate and selfish needs. Those tendencies have governed much of the legislation of the past, but their action was less injurious when they operated through a single class or through several but mutually qualifying classes than they would be if they worked in and through the collective people. We are face to face, then, with what we may truly call the supreme moment of our history. It is the people that now rule, and unless God live in and rule through the people, the end of all our struggles, the goal of all our boasted progress, will be chaos,— and chaos is death.

2. The sovereign people, then, ought not to be sovereignless; but their only possible sovereign is the God who is Lord of the conscience. His is the only voice that can still the noise of the passions and the tumult of the interests. This does not mean that His sovereignty is needed to be, as it were, a bit and

bridle by which they can be ridden or driven with greater ease; nor does it mean that its real or exclusive organ is a hierarchy or an organized clergy or official priesthood; but it does mean that the belief in an Infinite Majesty who reigns over all peoples and all persons, and to whom all are, now and eternally, responsible, needs to be worked into the very substance of the commonwealth and made, as it were, its common soul. And this work lies upon the Church as an imperative duty.

Without "the common people" who heard its Founder and Head gladly, it is depotentiated and impoverished. Its wealth lies in the souls it loves and teaches to love. Its function is to enrich their time with the ideals of eternity. And churches composed exclusively of rich or poor mean the reign of the conditions and categories of time within the realm of the Eternal. A labour church is a creation more of despair than of hope, an attempt, as it were, to sanctify an evil rather than to cure it. The terms "Master" and "Servant," "Capital" and "Labour" denote relations the Church ought not to know, and may not recognize, and to embody such distinctions in her very name is but to run up the flag of surrender. She carries for all mankind the noblest inheritance of our race, the wealth of divine love and grace, of human faith and hope and devotion, of saintly memory and heroic achievement, and only as she makes the inheritance she carries the possession of the common people, does she fulfil the end for which she was created.

RELIGION IN HISTORY

"We treat God with irreverence by banishing Him from our thoughts, not by referring to His will on slight occasions. His is not the finite authority or intelligence which cannot be troubled with small things. There is nothing so small but that we may honour God by asking His guidance of it, or insult Him by taking it into our own hands, and what is true of the Deity is equally true of His Revelation. We use it most reverently when most habitually. our insolence is in ever acting without reference to it, our true honouring of it is in its universal application."—Ruskin, "Seven Lamps of Architecture," Introduction.

"To those who act on what they know, more shall be revealed, and thus, if any man will do His will, he shall know the doctrine whether it be of God. Any man, not the man who has most means of knowing, who has the subtlest brains, or sits under the most orthodox preacher, or has his library fullest of most orthodox books,—but the man who strives to know, who takes God at His word, and sets himself to dig up the heavenly mystery, roots and all, before sunset, and the night come, when no man can work Beside such a man, God stands in more and more visible presence as he toils, and teaches him that which no preacher can teach—no earthly authority gainsay. By such a man the preacher must himself be judged."—Ruskin, "Notes on the Construction of Sheepfolds," "On the Old Road," ii. §§ 201, 202.

"We do not at all know everything which we have Luther and the Reformation in general to thank for. We have become free from the fetters of spiritual narrowness, we have, because of our progressive culture, become capable of returning to the source and apprehending Christianity in its purity. We have regained the courage to stand with firm feet on God's own earth, and to feel within us our human nature God-endowed Let spiritual culture continue ever to advance, let the natural sciences grow ever broader and deeper, and the human spirit enlarge itself as it will,—yet beyond the majesty and moral culture, which shines and lightens in the Gospels, it will not advance."—Goethe, "Eckermann's Gesprache," Dritter Th., pp. 372-373.

I

WHAT IS RELIGION?

CLEAR ideas are always necessary to intelligent discussion; but clear ideas are very hard to get, especially about the most familiar things. As a rule, what everybody is thought to know, nobody is found to understand. Now religion is one of the most familiar of things. We think, or hear, or speak, or read about it every day. Many are instructed in it every week of their lives. Yet were the question, What is religion? suddenly submitted to every man here, can you conceive what precisely would be the character of the answers? It is hardly too much to say that the variety, the contradictions, the confusion, the bewilderment, would be something wonderful, and most wonderful in the case of the men who thought that they understood the matter best and were quite prepared to put the perverted intelligence of the world right. To go to church, to go to chapel, to do Sunday School work, to read the Bible, to hold the faith of a given church, to observe its customs, to confess to the priest, to respect the parson, to agree with the minister, to believe in another world which has no concern with this, to be good, to do good, to love the society of good people—these, and such-like, might probably be found among the definitions.

Now whether these do, or do not, fairly represent current ideas, one thing, and one thing only, is meant to be here perceived, this, viz., that if we start with different ideas as to what the term religion means, we shall never understand each other's meaning or mind, never at any point of the reasoning become intelligible to each other, and so shall never by any possibility be able to reach a common agreement. Men may use the same word to express not only unlike, but opposite ideas, and if language be so employed it becomes a vehicle or means of hiding, not of communicating thought. Speech so used can only confuse and bewilder the judgment. Hence it is necessary at the outset of the discussion that we clearly and distinctly understand what the term "Religion" means. If we can do this, much is gained. You may not agree with my meaning or my mind, but at least you will be in a position to understand my arguments and judge the cogency or otherwise of any train and process of reasoning. In the world of thought, mischief is caused more by confusion than by any other cause. Not otherwise than by clear thinking can man reason to any purpose or reach any clear and sound conclusion.

Now I must begin by frankly bespeaking your patience. It is a hard matter to make intelligible abstract and abstruse things. You are many of you men accustomed to manual toil; I am a man accustomed to mental toil. I should be very much astonished and bewildered at the simplest processes of your daily work. You would have need to be patient in explaining the matter to me; and I often might be so stupid as not to understand the veriest rudiments of your craft. And so you may not at once see the issues and modes of a mental craft, that has occupied a man for many years more hours a day than any trades-union would allow him to work—has kept him hard at it in the early morning, at noon, and at night, until his subject may have become so much a matter of daily expression and association to him that he is unable really to estimate the difficulty of comprehension on the part of others not accustomed to the same methods and the same themes. Pardon me, then, if, to-night in particular, I occasionally become somewhat abstruse, and not as lucid as you would like me to be; but as we are concerned this night with the principles that underlie our whole argument, I must ask you to labour strenuously to comprehend these, that the later and more familiar discussions may have their proper place and force.

I

Our question then is, "What is religion?" Now it is best to begin by clearing our minds. You know Dr. Johnson's advice, "Clear your mind of cant."

Now the cant it is needful to clear our minds of is the confused thought that may stand in the way of clear comprehension. To this end let us at once note this—the relation of the churches to religion, of religion to the churches. Now, many people, perhaps most people, look at religion through the churches, and cannot understand it apart from them. To many, church is religion, and religion is church. Religion is the Church's concern. What it does is the religious. What it does not do is secular, or profane, or outside religion. What it condemns is irreligious. Well, many, so thinking, set down all the good religion has done to the churches; while others, so thinking, set down all the evil the churches have done to religion. Books have been written, speeches are daily made, to show how mischievous the action of the churches has been; and, therefore, how mischievous the action of religion. The churches have often been on the side of the rich and against the poor; the churches have often been on the side of tyranny and against freedom; the churches have often repressed liberty of thought, and hindered free discussion; the churches have often produced churchmen who have been fond of place, fond of power, fond of wealth. And all these things have been set down to the discredit of religion—the sins of the churches been made its sins, the evil of the churches its evil. Now, I mean to reverse that process, and look at the churches through religion, not at religion through the churches. They exist for it; it does not exist for them; they are to be judged as they are faithful to it; it is not to be condemned because they are unfaithful to their own great purpose and own great mission. Often the hardest obstacle to the realization of religion has been a church. An unfaithful servant may ruin a master; a church unfaithful may discredit religion. The great point, therefore, is to find what relation exists between these, that the one may be rightly conceived in its ideal perfection, and the other rightly judged in its historical sin or imperfection.

Let me illustrate what I mean. In Europe you have various types of polities. There is the imperial, absolute as in Russia; modified as in Austria, elective as in Germany. Then you have the monarchical running through various degrees; personal as in Prussia, constitutional as in Italy, and constitutional and limited—very limited indeed—as in England. Then you have the republican, young as in France, centuries old as in Switzerland. Now do you identify these polities with the peoples that dwell under them? or do you distinguish the two, studying the polities and judging them in relation to the peoples? The polities that do most to maintain law and order and to distribute impartial justice, that really represent the people, that help the just distribution of capital and wealth, that do most to promote the happiness, the progress, the freedom, of their peoples, are judged by you to be good; but the polities that fail to secure these things are judged by you to be bad, and bad in proportion to their failure. You do not judge the people through the polity; but you judge the polity through the people. If the polity be bad you do not pronounce condemnation on the people, but you pity them; you are gentle to them in proportion as the system from which they suffer is severe. Now as polities stand related to peoples, churches stand related to religion. The best polity is the polity that best secures highest material and social welfare; the best church is the church that secures most perfect realization for the ideal and spiritual—that is, the eternal, contents of religion. That polity which fails to do justice to the ideal of man is bad. That church which fails to do justice to the ideal of religion is not good.

But you will perceive that we have fixed an important principle. Religion is not to be looked at or judged simply from the churches. The churches are to be judged by religion. Again I say, they exist for it; it does not exist for them. They are good as they realize it; bad as they fail in realization. But that involves two points; first the utter futility and folly of condemning religion through and because of the churches; the utter injustice of identifying it with their imperfections and evils, or even holding it responsible for them. If a polity wrongs a people, depraves and hurts it, you don't declare that all government ought to cease; nay, you say, Let a government be created that shall do justice to the people, and help it to realize all the best possibilities within it, the whole ideal of society and of man it may contain. So, if you find imperfections in churches, do not use them as occasions to condemn religion ; use religion as a law or standard to condemn these imperfections, and insist that perfect churches alone can do justice to perfect religion. Then here is the next and second point : you must have a positive idea of religion before you can have a standard by which to judge the churches. The standard by which you judge a polity is the supreme good of the people. It depends upon your idea of the people's good how you judge the polity. But it is only a very recently recognized principle, this of the happiness of the people as supreme good. Old maxims were maxims like these : whose the region, his the religion ; the divine right of the king to rule, the divine duty of the people to obey, so making people exist for king, not king for people. We now understand, thanks to agencies which will be discussed later, that the grand purpose of all government is to promote the highest weal of the people ; that being reached, we can easily by due discussion determine the best form of polity and institution. So when we have got at the idea of religion we shall be able to determine in what way, by what methods, according to what polity, along what lines, churches must serve religion in order that they may serve the cause of God and of man.

II

We have got then the length of seeing this point: that the churches exist for religion, and are to be judged purely by their capability or power of realizing it. It is not to be held responsible for their imperfections; nay, these are to be judged by its perfection. But that only, as we see, throws us back upon the question with which we started—What is religion? But now, if we are to answer that, we must do so not only in a clear way, but in a large way; for mark!—man is a religious being. Look to the north and south, the east and west, and what do you see? religions! Wherever you turn—man; wherever man—religion. "No," says some very wise person, "not at all; there are low tribes, far down in the scale, found without any religious customs, without any religious ideas; religion is not universal." Well, I will not discuss the matter, but will only say this: the greatest ethnographers,—that is, the men who have most extensively studied the customs, the manners, the beliefs of men,—are on my side in affirming the opposite. But I do not stand on that. If you insist on it, let us grant that there are low tribes without religion. What then? Why this: to be without it is to be fallen into utter savagery; to be without it is to have the sure and indelible mark of lost manhood and utter barbarism. A great and distinguished thinker, Schelling, wrote a great book, which started from this principle:—

Man in the very act of founding society realizes religion; without religion there is no society; at its root, in all its customs, throughout all its laws, religion runs; and society is only where religion has begun to be. And that is a simple, certain fact. No man who knows ethnography, sociology, or whatever he may call the science which deals with the origins of institutions and civilization, will question it for a moment. Society and religion, as it were, begin to be together. Man cannot become a social, and therefore a civilized, being until he has a religion.

But now that has brought us to this point—that religion, since as old and as universal as man, is natural to him. It does not need a miracle to create it; rather this may be said: its cessation would require a miracle, would need the de-rationalizing, or, if you like, the de-naturalizing, of man. That might, along a great variety of lines, be proved to you. It would not be so very difficult of proof either were time only granted; but this meanwhile may be said: —So consonant are religious ideas with man's nature that that nature has always been at its best, whether in the individual or in the nation, when the religious idea was purest and when the religious idea was strongest. That is a matter capable of historical proof, absolutely incapable of historical disproof. Peoples that have been great in art have been great, for what reasons? To the Greeks, the masters in this region of all time, art was religious — the temple, the sculpture that glorified the god, declared the excellency of religion. Peoples, too, that have been great in literature have been great through their religious ideas. Look at the Jews. They were at the largest when at home a small people—a very little handful; they were rude, they were unlettered in a sense, yet they created what, from the literary point of view, must be called the most extraordinary literature in the world. There is in India a wonderful literature, vast, immense; it begins with the hymns of the Rig Veda, about fourteen hundred years before Christ, and comes down through the great Epics and Law Books and Philosophers to the Puranas, works almost of our own day. And what marks it? Religious ideas, and here as elsewhere, the purer and sublimer the religious idea, the finer and nobler the literature; only when it is lost in mythical and idolatrous extravagance does the literature become foolish and depraved. The Chinese have a great literature. What marks it? It is the exposition of the religion and the rule by which they seek to live. The Greeks, too, at their highest, noblest moment: what sort of a literature did they make?—what marks it?—religious ideas, and those very ideas were the breath of life to the men who vanquished Persia and made the drama and the philosophy of Greece. But it is not matter of art and of literature only. Take politics, the collective life, the freedom, the ideals which have been realized in all the higher and nobler forms of collective and social being, whence have they come?

From religion; wherever there has been highest order, wherever there has been noblest freedom, wherever there has been a patriotism that did not fear to die and did not care to live, save in so far as it lived for fatherland and faith, there has also been as the factor and inspiration of all the rest, the reign of great religious ideas. It is a universal law. Man at his best, man at his noblest, has been so through the action and by the help of religious ideas.

We see, then, that religion is something natural; that religious ideas are inseparable from our kind, that human nature is at its best when most religious. Now what does a wise man do when he stands face to face with facts of this sort? Does he begin a polemic against the absurdity of all religious ideas because of the false forms into which some have been forced, and the base uses to which they have been turned? No; when he stands face to face with this natural universalism, he asks, Whence are our common and imperishable religious ideas? Why do they everywhere come to be? Why has man in history been what he has been? Why has he thought as he has thought? These are necessary questions; these are scientific questions. It it not enough to say, certain orders of ideas are incredible. There stands behind us man in his history, and the whole course of that history illustrates man's invariable, uniform, absolutely universal tendency to produce, or generate if you like, or evolve religious ideas, and to be, in the whole of his institutions and in all his social order, governed and determined by them. Why? that is the point—why? He only who is able to enter into the meaning of that why, and get a reason, has come within glimpse of understanding the question —What is religion; for what it is depends in great part upon why it is.

Now I am not going to pause very long on this matter—the why—though I would it were possible to do so. I stand at a point where the passion and studies of my lifetime all converge; such energy as belongs to me having through years, and anxious and laborious days, been directed to the study and comprehension of some of the great problems that here arise. And when I see the shallow way in which many a man who thinks himself wise—wise from reading current magazines or newspapers—talks about matters of this kind, I feel,—if he could only be made to pass through twenty years of hard work along given lines, he would get to know enough of the matter he talked about to keep him at least a more modest man. But that is a matter only by the way. There are two great questions that arise out of that "why is religion?"—the one philosophical, the other historical. The philosophical question asks the reason as to the existence, as to the coming into being, and as to the growth in history of religious ideas and religious customs; and seeking this reason, it comes to see, what all history makes manifest, that the production and growth of these ideas are inseparable from the genesis and evolution of the reasonable nature of man. For what is history? It is a great attempt to realize man's inmost mind. It is but the externalization of what lay contained in him and his spirit. You cannot find that anything comes into being without a reason. You create institutions; this town is full of them: infirmaries, societies, unions—all manner of institutions; what are they? The realization of ideas, created by ideas, by thoughts which imperiously demanded of man that he should so embody them. And it is the function of the philosophic historian, the man of science in the field of religion, to get by analysis at the whole history of the genesis of the ideas that create our religious institutions. He is not concerned simply about how they are, he asks why they are, and traces them back into man, where mind acts and dwells. But what is so native and necessary to man is no matter of chance or accident; it is there of purpose; it was built into his nature by his Maker. And what the Creator thus purposed appears everywhere in and with the creature.

So much for the philosophical question, but the historical is quite as vital. It is a comparative one, concerned with all the religions of man. It puts the actual, extant, existing religions together, and compares them; and, comparing them, proceeds on the same scientific principle that comparative anatomy recognizes when it sees begin in the leaf the structural plan or purpose which finds its culmination in the glorious form and moving image of man. And so you find running through the religions a structural principle. Where that principle stands highest, in its greatest perfection, there and there only have you a perfect religion.

III

Now you see that this second discussion has carried us beyond the principle which was the conclusion or deduction from our first. Since man is unable to escape from religion, that which stands highest and is the best has most claim on his acceptance. Mark this—the people that has conceived the best idea of a commonwealth is the people farthest on the way to its realization, and the people that has the most perfect or the ideal religion has the greatest, the humanest, the wealthiest of all possessions, for it is the condition of every other ideal good. But there is another point involved in this second discussion. Religion is no affair of the churches. They did not create it. It created them. It is a great fact of nature, rooted in nature, growing out of nature, indissolubly connected with the whole system of nature or order to which man belongs. It is impossible for man to be, and yet to be without religion—observe, I say man, not men. Now, so much being determined by our two discussions, we are only the more completely and absolutely thrown back on our old question— What is religion, this universal, this natural, this inalienable possession of man? We must get a large idea ; and we must get a clear idea. Now perhaps the best way for me to proceed in attempting to answer this question will be by looking at the opinions of some great men concerning it, and in order to be perfectly fair and impartial it will be best to drop theologians out of account. Theologians may be dangerous : they may be, as it were, counsel retained for the defence. Well, we will ask, Are there any philosophers who can help us? Yes, many ; for it is a mark of our best modern philosophers that they feel that they must face and answer this question—why is religion ? and what is it ? You know the old deist who lived last century was a very remarkable man. He thought he could make what he called a religion of nature; but then you see he made that religion out of his own nature ; and his nature was not Nature's nature, but one that had been largely educated, civilized, refined, in a word, Christianized. As a result his religion was a purely ideal thing, a creation of his own consciousness, which had in its turn long passed out of a state of nature, and therefore could not make a natural in the sense of a primitive or aboriginal thing ; but what we want from the philosopher is not an ideal construction of that kind. We want to know what religion is, why it is universal, and what function it has to fulfil in the life of the individual and of the race.

Now there are two points of view from which the question may be discussed—the subjective and the objective, or religion conceived through man and religion in relation to man. We begin with the subjective, or more philosophical, for the function of a philosopher is this :—He seeks to explain what is or what comes to be through the nature of man, through the reason or the subjective personal capabilities of men. A philosopher is a lover of wisdom, and he goes in search of his wisdom not into the world without, but into the world within. But now it may astonish you —yet it is true—if I say that all knowledge of the world without is built on or involves a philosophy of the world within; and every natural science implies a given philosophy of knowledge and is determined to be what it is, not by its own processes, not by its imagined results, but entirely and absolutely by the relation in which it stands to thought, to knowledge, and therefore to the science concerned with what knows. Well, then, we will ask these philosophers to help us, and we shall find them so explaining religion that they fall into three classes—those who have tried to explain it through the intellect; those who have tried to explain it through the feelings; and those who have tried to explain it through the conscience.

First, then, those who have tried to explain it through the intellect; and three writers come here. One man says it is a matter of belief—altogether of belief, and not at all of reason. Jacobi, a distinguished German, said, "I believe; by my faith I am a Christian; by my reason I am a heathen." Now that man's theory is worth nothing, and I will tell you why. Any theory that leaves a division in a man's own soul is false. If religion be a mere matter of faith, unable to bear the light of reason, it is untrue to the nature the Creator gave the man. The second theory said, it is a matter of intuition; men, without proof direct, by action of intuitive reason, see the truths that constitute religion. This was Schelling's view, but he erred, and for this reason: a man's intuition may be sufficient for himself, but if made authoritative for other men, it is only dogmatism; it is his own affirmation of what he knows made to have universal validity. The third writer is Hegel. He said, "Religion is a matter of thought, of spirit." Now Hegel stood in this position:— People say that we have knowledge of phenomena. They forget that knowledge is not phenomenal. Phenomena are what appear. Take away the subject to whom they appear, and where are your phenomena? Seek to find a world where there is no thought, and you will never find any world at all. You can never reach a point where thought is not. Thought ever is the principle alike of the intelligence and the intelligible; without it man cannot interpret nature, nor could nature be interpreted. Hence it is implied in all things scientific, for the scientific is simply the intelligible. And the thought which makes science makes also experience possible; and thence comes this very vast but most valid deduction: as behind all experience thought lies, so at the root of the universe thought is. What is necessary to explain me, is necessary to explain nature. I am thought, and since phenomena can be only as thought is, then the reason or consciousness which is the condition of their existence, cannot be itself one of them. Nature, then, can be only as thought makes nature, underlies it, and builds it into an order or system. And that is apparent, for you can interpret nature only where you can take thought out of it, that is, only where you find the thought that is intelligible to your intelligence. There is not a language on earth that is not capable of allowing translation into any other language. This capability of being translated is the distinction between language and gibberish. You can take thought out of Greek and put it into English; you can take thought out of English and put it into Sanskrit; you can take thought out of Sanskrit and translate it into all the languages man has ever spoken. But what is the necessary condition? That thought be in the language. Where there is no thought, there can be no translation, nor can there be any language. There must be reason within in order that reason may be got out; and what is true of language is true of nature. Man could not get any natural science, could not get any knowledge of nature, unless nature were the great speech, the great language, an articulate and definite expression of thought. And as thought is the very medium in which reason lives and moves, religion as something rational has to do with thought, is our thought of the ultimate Being or Reason, and of our relation to Him. It is a matter of the Spirit within us and its relation to the Spirit without us ; it is the thought wherein man, the individual, places himself in relation to the universal—the intelligence in me to the intelligence that underlies all things.

But now we come to the second class of explanations. "Feeling," said the only theologian to whom I shall here allude, though he was quite as much a philosopher as any member of the band, "Feeling is the source of religion, a feeling of dependence." Now, you will note, a feeling of dependence is a thought of dependence. I cannot feel that I depend on anything or any one unless I think of myself as dependent. Without thought of the Independent upon whom the dependent self depends, no feeling of dependence is possible. Thought is contained in feeling. But another and specifically English thinker, with a similar idea, but as it were differently complexioned, has attempted to reconcile science and religion on the basis that worship, which is the essential element in religion, is feeling, the feeling of admiration. To admire is to worship ; to worship is to be religious. But, now, you cannot have admiration unless you have found something admirable ; and if you have found something admirable, you have conceived it, you have thought it ; you cannot have admiration without thought. Lastly, in this connexion, there comes that intellectually wise man, Mr. Herbert Spencer, who says, "Religion is a feeling, a feeling of wonder, a feeling of wonder in the presence of the Unknown." Now I don't wonder at his thinking wonder the root and essence of religion. I would, when his first principles are considered, have wondered exceedingly had he thought otherwise. It would be altogether inexplicable were a man to think that any other emotion whatever could be excited by the great Unknown. It is no extraordinary thing that a man who translates the Unknown by force, persistent force, should think that wonder was the one fit feeling, the feeling in any way proper to religion, that could arise in its presence. But you see he does not get his feeling till he has got his thought; you must conceive that the Unknown is before you can wonder at it. Yet the most wonderful thing of all is his theory as to the historical genesis of the feeling. He derives the feeling after the supersensible, after the divine —whence?—out of visions, seen in sleep, ghosts that have appeared in what we can only describe as the nightmares of a benighted and over-fed savage. Now if aught shows how men build theory without facing fact, it is a theory of this sort. There is not a historical religion in the whole world, save one, the Egyptian, that lends countenance to it, and that one, rightly understood, does not. All the rest, in China, India, through all Asia, in Europe, in Africa, with the one exception I have just named, and in America, all absolutely rise up and refuse to own it. The surprising thing, indeed, is that a man claiming to be a sociologist should seek to explain religion by phenomena that no historical religion, with the proverbial exception which proves the rule, recognizes as of primary importance.

Well, let us dismiss feeling as by itself, in any sense or degree, an adequate explanation of either the origin or nature of religion. All feeling means thought; you cannot feel unless you think; and you feel as you think. Then there is the next class of theories; and of these I will only mention two. One of them makes conscience the great mother of religion; or, religion is our duty apprehended as a Divine command. That is Kant's view; and the second is like unto it, only expressing by the outer sign the inward source—its author being the distinguished Englishman, Matthew Arnold. He describes religion as morality touched by emotion. But mark this:—You cannot have morality without thought. Thought underlies all, and is generic, while the others are only specific. Now religion is thought; it is feeling; it is action. It is not one of these. Yet it is all these, and something more. Man thinks; as he thinks, he feels, as he thinks and feels, he acts. Thought is the parent, determinative of feeling; feeling is the source of the motive which impels to act—that is, is the occasion of action, not its cause.

Well, when we analyze this subjective definition, what do we find? That religion is, on the side of the person, his thought of the cause, or order, or highest law under which he stands, and the way in which he feels and acts towards him or it. That is a very wide definition. We shall fill it up by and by. But I will indicate to you why it is so wide. It is wide for this reason: that it must comprehend all forms of religious expression or life that we may discover to exist. These have wonderful affinities. There is an African bending down before a fetish. He offers it a bribe; or perhaps he tries the opposite policy and castigates it—why? He thinks it can have influence for good or for evil on his life, and so he seeks to secure the good and prevent the evil. There, again, is John Stuart Mill. He says, speaking of the woman who became his wife: "Her memory became to me a religion, and her approbation the standard by which, summing up as it did all worthiness, I endeavour to regulate my life." So, the thought, the memory, and imagined approbation of his wife, became a religion. It was the religion by which he ordered his life. In both there is a given notion or conception of the position occupied and the influence exercised, in the one case, by a thing, which is yet conceived to be so alive as to be susceptible to flattery or abuse, in the other, by a dead woman, who yet lives as a moral ideal; and there results, on the one hand, the emotion here of fear, there of love, while, on the other hand, there is action, the sort of action the spirit which is in the thing or the woman who is idealized, is supposed to approve.

Then there is the Chinaman who has great ideas of his ancestors, the ancestral spirits. He has a large calendar of saints, and a great hall where the sages of the past stand. He believes that all his people constitute a mighty organic whole, and he propitiates the spirits of the dead that he may live a happy and a dutiful life. It is a long cry from China to France; yet Comte's notion of the worship of humanity, with its sages and calendar of saints, with much of its outward pomp and worship, is but the ancient Chinese thought amplified by baptism into the rites and associations of the Catholic Church. Our wide notion of religion enables us to comprehend under it systems as distant and dissimilar as these.

IV

Now, when we have got a notion of religion on the subjective side, we want another of it on the objective; and here I must pray your simple attention.

1. Looking, then, at religion on the objective side, we may say, that the character of its highest conception—*i.e.* the course or order or highest law under which man conceives himself to stand—determines its nature and quality; or, in other words, the highest conception which a religion possesses determines its moral character. A bad god can never have a good religion. As is the deity, such must the faith that is built on him be. Find out

then the character of the deity, and you find out the character of the religion. In other words, discover the quality of a man's highest thought, and you discover the character and quality of the principles that regulate his whole life. That is absolutely true. You may take it of religion; you may take it of any intellectual system. Suppose, for example, that a man declares force to be the ultimate, or the only known ultimate of ultimates, how would it affect his notion of life and the law that governs conduct? First, I would ask you to consider whence the man got his idea of force. If you take mind away, what is force? A man tells me, "I know only phenomena." Let me ask him, are you then a phenomenon? Are you? For if you are, then see this: phenomena can never determine each other; they may co-exist but they do not produce and govern one another; they must be determined or governed by something real. To speak in English, not in Greek—things can appear only provided there are those to whom they appear. Take away the persons for whom are appearances, and where, pray, are the appearances? But, secondly, without going into metaphysics, let us see this: if a man postulates force as his highest thought, the primary or ultimate cause of all that is known, what follows? Force, according to its very idea, must exact in every change an equivalent for what is expended. Wherever force rules, the laws of mechanics rule, wherever the laws of mechanics rule, necessity rules; wherever necessity rules, freedom is absent; wherever freedom is absent, morality is impossible; wherever morality is impossible, duty is impossible, and all the varieties of service into which and through which a noble and ordered society can be constructed. The highest conception thus determines the whole order of thought. Now that idea of force, or the idea of creation that it is thought to translate, is a very old idea. The ancient Hindus knew it; and it is only an unconscious translation of Hindu thought into an ill-fitting English garb. Thousands of years ago it stood in Sanskrit, clear and unmistakable, in more scientific form than it has in English to-day, with results which it is hoped later lectures may make abundantly manifest.

2. But, if you apply the principle—as is the highest thought, so is the system—to religion, you get this conclusion: if you have a God absolutely righteous, absolutely holy, absolutely loving, all the system He creates or builds must be intended to conform to Him. But, simply because he is so spiritual and moral, its absolute conformity cannot be secured by any mechanical method. If it were made conformable by a mechanical method, this would mean that it was done by necessity, and necessity destroys morality; and hence we must qualify and complete our first by a second principle —the method and medium by which God secures conformity to Himself must be as moral as He Himself is: in other words, while God is the great determinative idea of religion, religion itself must

always be realized through man. It must, I say, be realized through man—man free, rational, intelligent. Man stands open to God, God speaks through man. The pure in soul see and hear Him. Did you ever hear an oratorio? Who made it? Nature never made it, nor could she by herself alone take one step towards its making. Yet nature to the susceptible ear is full of sounds, soft, loud, low, sweet, murmuring, gentle, varied, is a very orchestra of musical, rhythmical sounds ; and the master spirit gathers into his vast imagination all these sounds, weaves them into splendid harmonies, and pours them out in the great organ swell, or the vast choir made of human beings, who yet make music as if they were one. And so the spirit open to God, God's true prophet, is the great master spirit telling the truth of God for the joy and the life of men.

3. But this brings us to a third position. Since religion, while it comes from God, is yet realized through men, it is realized for the purposes of God. It exists for His ends, and for these alone. Now, in looking at it as a great agent for carrying out God's purposes, what do we see? Two things. First, religion has a power that nothing else has of making bad men good. There is no power like it for changing bad into good, the profane into the holy, the man unreal into the man most true. Science has not that power ; nor has art. Science and art witness to the elevation of man; they do not cause it. Religion causes the elevation of man, and creates his

science and his art. Secondly, the progress, the forward movement of the race of man, has been worked by good persons, persons made good by their religious ideas. That is an absolute law. Sometimes there is a sneaking kindness in the heart of a people in a certain stage of growth or decay for a statesman who is a brilliant scoundrel, because they conceive him to be a great, or an astute genius ; but, when the reins of a state are in the hands of a brilliant scoundrel, the state is being driven right into the heart of a great evil, or some signal misfortune. It is only the good person that can create really good things ; and so we may add, wherever you have persons, whether inside or outside Christianity, that lift men up, and send men forward, you find them persons inspired by religious ideas.

And now we must from these positions draw what may be termed a provisional conclusion :— Since the great forward movement of the world is worked by religious persons, then the higher their thought the greater and more beneficent their power ; the purer the idea that works in them and through them, the greater and grander will be the religion. I will not by comparison run through Brahmanism, through Buddhism, through Islam, through Egypt, through Greece ; I will not try by comparison to show where this grandest idea is. But I will ask you to think of God as the Saviour has taught us to think of Him, and then see how this bears on action. He is not only almighty, but He is good, holy, wise, loving, tender, compassionate, just. Take for example : God is a being infinitely good ; then He cannot but hate sin, He cannot but hate all conscious and voluntary guilt ; but if God hates sin, the religious man, governed by his idea of God, hates it too, and lives that he may end its reign on earth. God is righteous. Then if He is righteous, He cannot but hate wrong ; all forms of wrong, personal, social, industrial, political, are hateful to Him ; and the man who is a religious man, governed by his thought of God, must live to conquer wrong. God is tender, compassionate ; then all sorrow, all pain, and all anguish are to Him painful, the cause of deepest pity and regret ; and the religious man lives to overcome all pain, to subdue it, to minister to it ; to take the outcast, and the lonely, and the feeble, and the desolate into the protection of his great pity. God is love ; then He loves to see man saved, to see him happy, to see happiness multiplied below ; and so the religious man is the man who saves men, who creates happiness, who makes all earth a scene of wider joy and of grander moral worth. Theology is the interpretation of the universe through the idea of God. Religion is the regulation of life through the same great idea ; it is the application to all things, and all events, of the great, spiritual, moral, ethical, rational elements contained in that idea.

Now that description of religion has yet to be filled up. Historically we must deal with it later. This lecture alone cannot be either complete or perhaps, fully, intelligible, for it is only a vestibule, a hall, introducing you to what is within and behind. But even as the question now stands, mark this : religion has become no simple way of merely saving men ; it saves them—but for God's ends, not simply their own. It is no mere method for giving peace in death, or a happy immortality ; it accomplishes that by making time happy, and a happy society. Religion is in order that eternal justice, eternal holiness, eternal purity, eternal harmony, eternal love may, through man, be made everywhere to reign among men. Religion is that the purpose of God through all the ages may by men be more perfectly fulfilled. Where it comes in its perfection, it comes for ends like these. If religion be this, where is the man who would not be religious ?—and religious that he may serve God and work the good of man.

II

THE PLACE AND SIGNIFICANCE OF THE OLD TESTAMENT IN RELIGION

LAST Sunday evening we were mainly concerned with principles, with an attempt to fix the ideal or standard for judgment in our discussions on religion. Without such a standard we cannot be just; can neither rightly understand, nor fairly estimate, the action of religion in history. Justice is always discriminative, and the man who has neither the patience nor the mind carefully to sift a matter to the bottom, and distinguish what does, from what does not, belong to it, is not fit to be a judge. But the judge needs more than a discerning judgment. He needs an impartial mind and a standard or norm, both moral and legal, by which to test or measure the guilt or innocence of the person he tries. That impartial mind no man can give to another; he must by earnest repression of passion and prejudice, by diligent criticism of his own temper and motives, by cultivation of simple and honest love of truth, gain it, and keep it for himself. Goethe said, "I can promise to be sincere, but I cannot promise to be impartial." Controversy may be sincere, but justice must be both sincere and impartial, and without justice no judgment can be just.

Well, then, it is your part to cultivate and to exercise the impartial mind; it was mine to attempt to formulate the standard or ideal that should regulate judgment; in other words, the law according to which you were to be asked to judge. That standard or law was the idea of religion. That its significance may be seen, it may be necessary to recall it, or rather, the steps in the discussion that led up to and culminated in it.

Note, then, religion is not Church. The churches are our means, or associations, or agencies, for its realization, good so far as efficient, bad in the degree that they are inefficient. If in their teaching they misinterpret its truths, if in their action they pervert or misrepresent its spirit, then, however loud their speech, however high their claims, they are irreligious, mischievous in proportion to their strength. While religion is no creation of the churches, it is the highest concern of man, universal as man, necessary to his nature, inseparable from it, needing no miracle to create, in need rather of a miracle to uncreate, it. Since universal as man, every true science and philosophy of man must seek to understand his religions, must find their reason or cause in him, and in the system to which he belongs; must find, too, that since necessary, the most perfect is the best religion for man, needed to perfect or complete his nature.

But, then, if religion be universal, by what terms may it best be expressed or defined? Neither in those of thought or feeling, or action, but by some notion large enough to combine the three. So it was described as man's thought as to the cause or order or highest law under which he stands, and the way in which he feels and acts towards him or it. Now, that definition was wide enough to comprehend the most distant and dissimilar religions. But, then, it remains empty till it be supplemented by an objective analysis. Now, that analysis revealed three points:— first, that in a religion the supreme idea was the determinative idea, viz., the thought, or conception of God, or what was made a substitute for Him. A bad god never had a good religion; as man thinks of his deity, so is he and so is his religion. But, secondly, while God was the determinative idea, religion was realized through men, and conditioned by the men through whom it was realized. And, thirdly, while realized by men, it was, as proceeding from God, a means to His ends. Hence the better the god, the better the means and the nobler the end. In short, the religion is the conception or idea of God applied to the ordering of life, and to the organization of society. If God be the absolutely good, supreme in all goodness, then to say that a religion worthy of Him exists, is just to say that life will be ordered and society organized according to the highest possible ideal.

Now, this restatement and summary of the previous

lecture is needed for two reasons in particular—first, to show what was not intended. There was no attempt at argument for the existence of deity, no endeavour after a constructive theism. Had I intended to prove the being of God, I should have gone to work in another method, along other lines, although they might have touched at one point the argument of last evening. It was the idea of religion, not the idea of God, that was under discussion; and so, secondly, the purpose was to explicate and formulate principles that should regulate judgment concerning it. We are about to study certain religions in history; but we cannot understand their character and action, unless we have a true and clear idea of what religion is as regards origin and essence and nature. That idea being formulated, the principles are expressed that are to be our standard, our ideal, applied or implied, in all our after discussions.

I

1. Our study, then, is the study of certain religions in history, first that of the Old Testament, and next, that of the New. Now it ought to be possible to make that a scientific study, scientific in method, purpose, spirit, and it will be this, if we are able, in the brief time at our disposal, to discuss the precise action of these great religions in the history and social progress of man. But this is a scientific study for a pre-eminently practical purpose. It is

the duty of all men to seek for the truth, for only so is it to be found; but it is no less the interest of every man to discover what ideas and influences have been, in the long and varied life of our race, morally and socially healthful, and what morally and socially injurious. It must be to the advantage of every person to know the good ; it can be to the profit of no one to maintain the pernicious or bad. For here we are all of us, in our own order and place, workers; we work by hand or brain, we work at the desk or in the mill, in the library or in the laboratory. And what we, as men who work, want to know, is this, what are the best principles for organizing society, for helping the creation of personal wellbeing, and no less for the making of the common weal, and so for the forming of a true commonwealth. Now, there is only one way in which we can do this with any real advantage ; we must study man in history, that we may discover the great forces that have been the great factors of these results. It is only through the study of history, scientifically pursued, that we can find out what ideas and agencies have most worked for good, have, by their action alike on the individual and on collective society, best served the progress, the peace, the wellbeing of the race.

Now, I confess, frankly and at once, that the truths of the religions of the Old and New Testaments are to me the ideas that have worked most creatively, beneficently, and progressively in history, have above all others brightened and enriched the lot of the men who toil. But let me also add, you are not to be asked to believe this on my word, but only so far as it is by history and argument scientifically proved. I must ask you to come to the inquiry with free and unprejudiced minds. You know dogmaticism is not peculiar to men who believe ; it is often more characteristic of men who disbelieve. You may almost any day find the most arrogant, because the most ignorant, dogmaticism disguised as scepticism— indeed, I will venture to say you will find more in a week's issue of the so-called free thought press than in all the decrees of the council of Trent. All that I wish is the open mind, not the spirit that looks into the past only that it may find a weapon with which to beat the present, but the spirit only anxious to discover the beliefs that have most worked for human good. To such a spirit, and only to such, is a scientific study of religion in history possible.

But what makes a study scientific ? It is the method, the way in which it is done. Scientific study in the field of history simply means, a skilled man working in a skilled way for the discovery of the truth. Nothing is here possible without skill, and skill gained by long and hard and patient work. No man can gain it by reading a few books and making them his authorities. He must go to the fountain-head himself. That man, and that man alone, can use the scientific method, who has steeped his spirit to the very core in the thought and mind of the people, the times, the literature, the religion, he seeks to understand and make understood. A man who knows both to-day and the past finds it difficult to be just to the past, but to the man who knows only to-day, justice is not at all possible. If you read the past as you read the columns of a newspaper, and judge it as you judge our current literature, if you carry back into it the opinions, associations, standards, and conflicts of to-day, then you study it as a prejudiced polemic or a pitiful controversialist, not as a scientific student. And what will be the result? Why, you will never get at the truth, you will arrive instead only at falsehood and error; you will, besides, do the most frightful injustice to the past and inflict the utmost injury on your own mind by persuading it that it is seeking for the truth, when the object of its search is really material for controversy.

But how, then, does the scientific student proceed? While enriched with the experience and critical insight centuries have been required to win, he so uses them as to look at the period he studies as it was amid its own lights and under its own conditions, judging it as a root, not as a branch of to-day. He follows history, watches its way, does not force it to take his. He does not think that to know a river you have only to look at it from the city that stands at its mouth, but he believes that to be scientific the explorer must ascend to its source, noting and measuring every rivulet that swells its waters. But to do this in history, what do you need? You need imagination, large scholarship, keen and earnest thought; so that you may, as it were, live in the past, and make it live its veritable life in the light of your own eyes. You must go back, say, into the Mosaic age, study Moses, study Egypt, study Mesopotamia, study Phœnicia, their peoples, their religions, their politics, their social state, their morals, their wealth and poverty and commerce; you must study, too, India, ancient through modern Arabia, the nascent Isles of Greece through their languages and mythologies;—and then, when you are full of all this knowledge, with your imagination quickened and kindled by it, you must construct the world as it then was, and apply to its peoples and their conduct, not yours, but their own moral standards and ideas. But you do this, not simply to know the given period, but to understand its contribution to the common good and progress of man. You thus compare the peoples, their laws, customs, religions, and religious ideas, in order that you may seek to find out where, and when, and why these laws, customs, religions, and religious ideas arose; and then, possessed of this comparative knowledge, you try to measure these things in their influence on the then present, in their influence on what was then future, in their power to affect for good their own age, and the ages that were still to come. The man who can go back and make an old religion live in its real historic being and relations, is the only man capable of applying the scientific method, either to religion or history.

2. Now, I am going to ask you to-night to look at only one religion, though we shall try to do so in this comparative way, the religion which has as its peculiar literature the Old Testament. I would it were here possible to apply to it in fullest measure the historical and comparative method. But to do so and bring it and all the religions of its time into comparison would take too many evenings from me, and would too much tax your thought and patience. A distinguished scholar, whose name is well known throughout Europe as almost the symbol for scientific inquiries on this field, said but two months ago to me, " If you want to prove the truth, the wisdom, the sober and honest history of the Bible, and the purity of its religion, place it among the Sacred Books of the East. In these books there are many grains of gold, but they are hid in mountains of the most extraordinary rubbish ; and the extraordinary thing is that it is the rubbish that calls forth the enthusiasm and admiration of the peoples that own them. The sobriety of the Bible, the purity of its spirit, the elevation and devotion of its tone, make it occupy an entirely unique place. Placed among the Sacred Books of the East the contrast would make its truth only the more stand out." While, however, it is here impossible to follow the comparative method, yet let me ask for the Book itself your earnest, impartial, careful consideration. To that, indeed, it has an indefeasible right. Simply as a piece of literature it is the most marvellous thing in the world. You

call it a Book, but it stands there a literature, the creation of from twelve to fifteen hundred years, in fragments, some small, others larger, each fragment reflecting its own age, the earliest being most dissimilar and strange to the latest; yet with all its distance, and all its variety, this Book is so modern, and stands so near to us, that it may be said to be of all the books in the world the nearest to our spirits. It contains, from the literary and moral points of view, the most remarkable code of ancient times. It contains the quaintest, most beautiful, and graphic history. It contains the supreme devotional literature of the world, the literature that men in their highest moments of religious transport or of pious meditation have used to express thoughts too deep for tears. It contains poetry that, simply as poetry, stands foremost in its own order, full of a great sense of mystery, full of an awful sense of suffering, pierced and transformed by a glorious sense of God. It possesses more than all a conception of God and an idea of man, without a parallel in the literature and religions of the ancient world. That Book is the noblest heirloom of humanity. To every man it belongs as an inalienable birthright. To its best truths, to its inmost heart, to its meaning, for this and for all times, you have all an indefeasible right. The worst of frauds were the act of the man who should cheat you out of it. The man who can use it only as the bone of a father wherewith to smite a son, only shows himself of the order of men who rush in where angels fear to tread.

Of course, I know what is said in certain organs of what calls itself free thought. There are sayings in the Old Testament that sound not too refined to our dainty and delicate modern ears. There are persons in it guilty of acts that, measured by modern standards, cannot be called good, but must be pronounced evil. There are statements in it that seem to conflict with our latest wisdom, or are out of harmony with our last new science. It is easy to bring up hundreds of the sort of difficulties which we find raised by men who study it from and on the polemical platform of to-day. Such men will tell you, in gravest tones, of difficulties fatal to the religious claims and character of the book, but when you come to examine them, they turn out to be the mere creatures of ignorance, formed out of a theory of the Bible and its religion, more akin to childish simplicity than to masculine intelligence. Before a true theory of its origin and meaning these difficulties could no more live than a man could breathe in a vacuum. Yet I feel tender to the man, so touching is his intellectual innocence, who would reject the Bible because of the doings of Jacob, the sins of David, or the perplexities in the history of Cain. His difficulties come to me like a reminiscence out of my own boyhood; his perplexities recall those that daily troubled the good and devout people amongst whom my earliest life was cast, only they had the wisdom to see that what perplexed them belonged to the incidents of the history, not to the essence of the religion.

But, now, instead of dealing with such things as if deserving of grave and detailed criticism, let me ask you a question, Do you think these difficulties explain the Bible, the power it has had, and still has? Do they help you to understand it better, or do they make it in any degree intelligible to you? Do they not when regarded as making it incredible, and unworthy of respect, rather make it and its influence utterly unintelligible? For, think, in making the Bible ridiculous, what is it you make ridiculous? It is not simply a Book—that were a small matter, but it is a race, nay, two races, the two that have done most for civilization, that have created it, that form the noblest flower and fruit of humanity. What makes the Bible ridiculous, makes man so; what makes man ridiculous, turns his history into the very march of unreason. You say, perhaps, " These things offend my conscience, and what offends my conscience I must condemn." Good ; they offend my conscience, and my conscience condemns them ; but to condemn the doings of Jacob or the sins of David is not to condemn the Bible, nay, is rather to vindicate it, for it did not record these things for our approval, but for our disapproval on the one hand, and for our personal instruction on the other. What conscience disapproves, ought not to be spoken of with approval, whoever or whatever may command us to do so. But before a man uses the judgment of his conscience on the acts of certain men or a certain nation as a reason why he should despise the Bible and reject its religion, ought he not to raise this prior question :—Whether he has got at the meaning of the book, and whether he understands the methods of its use? Think what the Bible has been to the devoutest and most pious of our race, the most moral, the most humane, the most gentle to men, the most obedient to God. Has it not been their inspiration for good, the power that has entered their lives and lifted them from the lowest of sensuous levels to the highest and noblest of spiritual ideals? And ought not this simple fact alone make our innocent objectors pause and ask, whether it is the Bible or their theory of the Bible that is at fault? whether it has been the fortune of their ignorance to find what knowledge missed, or whether there has befallen it the fate of the unskilled sailor, who has mistaken the ripple on a sandbank for the long roll of the Atlantic waves.

II

1. But these are mere introductory and formal questions; and we must hasten to others more radical and material. What concerns us is the place and the significance of the book in religion, and of its religion among religions. Now, note this self-evident and apparent distinction;—the book is the history of a religion, it is not a history which is a religion, and

it is with the religion and its history, and not simply with the book, that we are here concerned. I do not deny that reason, conscience, judgment, and all the faculties of criticism must be exercised upon and about the book, but it is less the book than its religion that we want to understand. And note, next, as the book is a history, or the materials for a history, so our concern with it relates not to questions in its literary criticism, but to the beginning or origin, the matter or nature, the growth, the progress, and the culmination of the religion. You have to study the religion in what it was, what it did, and what it became. In its course there is much mixed up with it that is historical setting, that belongs to place or time. But it is the kernel, the everlasting essence, the pre-eminent and abiding substance that here concerns us, not what by the way falls off and perishes.

Now, mark, the religion is said to come from God. That is not an incredible or irrational proposition: Nay, it is one that has the highest reason, though to attempt to demonstrate its reasonableness would lead us too far away from our proper subject. That revelation is possible is here, if not conceded, yet assumed. I do not speak to atheists. I do not speak as an atheist, but as a theist to theists. And now to say that God is, is simply to say that revelation is possible; to say that God is not, is simply to say that revelation is impossible. If He is, He must be free to act; if He acts, He must be free to stand in relation to man;

if He is free to stand in relation to man, He can speak to him, and through him. There is a theism that denies God in fact, though it affirms Him in words. The man who so limits God's activity as to prevent His action every moment and in relation to every man is no theist, but in the strict historical sense of the term a deist Deism set God at a great distance from nature and man. The world went according to its own laws, without any help from Him; indeed all such help was described as interference, or intervention, as it were a violation of law on the part of Him who made the law; but to me such a deism is only atheism in providence. As I conceive matters, the laws of nature are modes of God's action, they simply express His ceaseless activity. Man's relation to God is based on God's prior relation to man, and so, if the being of God be granted, manifestative or self-communicative action, or, in other words, revelation, and as a consequence, religion follows as a logical necessity, which only means a necessity in reason. Revelation and religion but express the continued activity of God; the idea of God regulates the history of the revelation and determines the character of religion. Since religion is from God but through man, man is the condition through which the institutive revelation comes But, coming through man, it partakes of the imperfect, the earthly quality of the vessel that bears it. To an absolutely perfect religion, you need an absolutely perfect vehicle Until you get the perfect vehicle, you have not, and cannot have, perfect religion.

Again, religion comes through men to make man perfect. Since it does not come to man as already perfect, it falls necessarily under the law of human progress. You cannot create a perfect moral character. A perfect physical creature may be created, but a perfect moral creature is incapable of creation. He must act, he must be disciplined, he must be taught; he is made perfect by the things which he suffers. He is like

> Iron dug from central gloom,
> And heated hot with burning fears,
> And dipt in baths of hissing tears,
> And batter'd with the shocks of doom
> To shape and use.

But this carries with it necessarily the position— since man is the vehicle or form through whom religion comes, then it begins to come to man in his least perfect moment in order that it may prepare him for a more perfect state. To think that the ideal of religion is at the earliest moment of its appearance already manifested in ideal men, is to have no historical sense, and so no faculty for the scientific study of history. It comes to the man, to the people, or the race, to make the man, the people, or the race, into the perfect beings they need to become. Primarily and necessarily the man is below the religion, but his elevation is ordered and measured by its development. The religion comes to lift the man. And so its history exhibits, on the one hand, a process in man and, on the other, a progress in idea and institution ; the process is the greater fitness of the vehicle, the progress is the greater perfection of the religion.

2. Now these statements and distinctions will help us to deal with the history of the religion which we believe to have come from God, but know to have been realized through man. It has, therefore, necessarily the imperfection of the form through which it comes, conditioning what belongs to the perfection of the source whence it proceeds. But from these more or less external questions, let us now advance to questions essential and central ; and note this—the distinctive, the great determinative principle in the Old Testament was the conception of God. And you must distinguish here between the conception and its history, what belongs to it by virtue of its own nature, and what belongs to its reflection in the minds and in the history of the men, or people to whom it came.

We shall take the conception first ; and here we must note that it was a new thing in the world. It came expressing faith in one God, a monotheism,— the parent of all other monotheisms. As it was the first it became the greatest and purest, and it expressed this pre-eminence in two emphatic ways, by name and by character.

(i.) By name. This age is greatly exercised to discover a name for the Primary Cause. It has been termed the Unconditioned, the Unknown, the

Unknowable, the Unconscious, the Infinite, negatives all without a single positive trait. But of all the names for the ultimate Cause or God ever discovered, the grandest yet most descriptive was that used by the old Hebrew men. Note that name—Jehovah, or Yahveh; Lord as it is given in our English version, or as the French give it, the Eternal. Now, if you resolve it into its original speech, what does it mean? Its meaning, though about it there have been many discussions, is yet clear. It must mean either He who is, or He who causes to be. It is then a verb, but it is a verb used as a proper name, He who causes to be, or He who is.

But apart from this all the older and earlier names of God came from one of two sources. First, they were borrowed from nature, its phenomena, processes, or events. Such were the Indo-European names, those of the stock to which we ourselves belong. Their names were all primarily physical terms, the earth, the sun, the blue heaven, the starry heaven, the great sea, the hills, the moon, the dawn, the sunset. These all provided names for God, but mark the result! The gods all partook of the qualities of the nature that supplied them with names; like it they were unstable, stormy, tempestuous, variable; they had a created and limited being, and were gifted with passions like men, so that when men stood in relation to them, it was as fully on a par or equality with them. And this followed—no people of our stock ever thought of God as a Creator, not one. Wise people in these days say, the idea of a cause created the idea of God. But we must recognise this plain historical fact, that not a single primitive god of the race to which we belong, from India to Western America, had the idea of creation associated with him. Every god was a created being, stood in the circle of nature, passionate, stormy, variable, manlike.

The second great source of divine names was Man, his political offices, metaphysical attributes or functions. God was called the strong, or the mighty; He was called the King, or the Lord, and men were his servants. Now, the stock of which the Jews came used names of this order, and what did the usage mean? That, as the King was, so was the god conceived to be, as was the Lord, so was the Almighty. In the East the despot reigned, and so God was thought to be arbitrary, cruel, bloodthirsty, propitiated by human sacrifice. In the East, kings cared not for men, but only and always loved power, even though bought by blood and death. And as were the kings such were the gods,—violent, despotic, prone to an anger that could be appeased only by blood.

These, then, were the old conceptions, but now came this new great conception:—God is not a multitude, He is one, and we call Him by no name that suggests man, by no name that suggests nature; we call Him—He who is, He who causes to be. He is one, beside whom is no fellow. He is a person; His "Thou" stands over against my "I," He is not caused, but He causes; is boundless, mighty, potent, powerful, personal, Jehovah. This name of God, this great and mighty name, could help men to think under other forms, in another and nobler fashion, of the great and supreme One.

(ii.) Now, note the next point—the character. The fundamental idea as to character stands expressed in the formula, "Be ye holy, for I am holy." God is holy, and only a holy man, only a holy people, can please Him. Therefore, the religious man must be a good man. "Of course," you say, "of course. We all expect a religious man to be a good man. The most pious ought to be the most honourable of men." But, pray, why do you expect him to be this? No heathen of antiquity ever expected any such thing. Piety had nothing to do with the general personal virtues; ethics were the concern of the schools and the poets, not of the temple and the priests. A religious man in the ancient world did not need to be a good man. Why, the gods themselves were not good,—often most utterly iniquitous and bad. In India, in the old hymns you could get written in honour of a god a drinking song that any man in these days in an hour of hilarity might fitly sing. In beautiful, skilful, radiant Greece, what was Zeus, their great god?—an adulterer; what was Aphrodite?—personified lust. If you had said to a Greek, you ought to be god-like, he would have said, "Nay, I will be man-like; that is more noble and honourable than to live after the manner of the gods."

And if you had gone east into Phœnicia where the neighbours of the Jews lived, what would you have found?—You would have found gods, impurest of the impure, served not only by human sacrifice, but by blackest, vilest, human lust. Religion was no moral thing then, in any degree whatever, and where it had power without morality its power worked in the most immoral way. Imagine then, the transcendent moment for man, the moment of supremest promise, of grandest hope, when the idea of a moral deity entered his heart, and passed into his history, when all the energies of religion came to be moral energies for the making of moral men. That was a moment, I call it, of revelation—you may call it of supreme guesswork or grandest discovery; or you may, by magnifying incidental difficulties, attempt to conceal from yourselves its meaning. Yet it were only to speak with prosaic soberness were we to say,—the moment when gravitation, navigation, the secret of the sea, of the sun, or the stars, or the earth, were discovered had neither singly nor all combined equal or even approximate significance for man. Take from the heart of him this religion steeped in morality, made living by the moral character of its God, and you will leave him without the grandest energy working for good and peace and progress that ever came into his history or into his heart.

3. Now let us see where we stand: we have got the distinctive character and quality of the new idea:—God is one, personal, supreme, self-existent,

a Being who can be named after no object in nature, and no attribute or office of man, but only as He who is or He who causes to be. And He is moral —high and severe in righteousness, He loves good and hates evil. As He is His people ought to be; no service but moral service can be acceptable to Him. Such, then, was the idea; but it was one thing to get it, another to translate it into reality and life. A generation may suffice for the one, but centuries are needed for the other. The ideal was of God, but the realization was through man, and we must distinguish what belonged to the perfect Source from what was proper and peculiar to the imperfect medium. The religion did not stoop to the level of the people, the people had to struggle up to the altitude of the religion, and their struggle was attended by many an error, many a fall, and many a wilful apostasy. Indeed, it remained ever far above them, and so proved its divinity, just as their failure proved their humanity. Consider what they were, and where they stood, when they received the religion of God and His law. Slaves, just escaped from Egypt, with the vices of their kind, ignorant, unstable, stubborn, impatient of freedom, accustomed to a cruel and crushing tyranny, rebellious under an authority too moral to coerce. Then, imagine them settled in their own land, undisciplined men, unfamiliar with an ordered life, with all the arts of peace to learn, surrounded by such religions as I have described, envious of the licence they allowed, anxious to be let sin as their neighbours sinned, and to conceive, appease, and please Jehovah as the other peoples conceived and appeased and pleased their gods.

Now, let me put two questions to you, how ought you to judge a people so placed? By the standards of our day, or of their own? And, again, how ought you to judge their religion,—through the people, or the people through it? In the first place, could you conceive a people so situated and so constituted, producing of their own mere will and out of their own poor nature such a religion? It stood in conflict with their habits, their passions, with all their circumstances, with what they most liked and most desired. Now, can that which stands in radical contradiction to a nature be a product of the nature it radically contradicts? In the next place, can you wonder that the religion and the people were often in collision? The collision was altogether to its honour—its standard being so high, but altogether in keeping with their nature, its tendencies and instincts being what they were. Yet why do you judge the Hebrews more harshly than you judge any other people of antiquity? I am not saying you are wrong in so judging, I am only asking the reason. They were not worse, they were better than their neighbours. Their kinsmen, the Arabs, were incomparably more cruel, treacherous, and bloodthirsty. The Phœnicians, kinsmen too, far richer and more cultivated, were proverbial for lust, lying, and greed, for a horrible lasciviousness that made them pollute every shore and people they touched. The Assyrians, also kinsmen, were tyrannous, ruthless, and exterminating to a degree that made them hated and feared throughout all the ancient world. Now, why are you so severe to the comparatively moral and inoffensive Hebrews, while you are silent as to the awful immoralities that made kindred and contemporary peoples a positive plague, causes of utmost disaster to their own and later times? Is it not because you expect more of the Hebrews, which surely can only mean that you judge them by a higher law? But why do you so judge them? Is it not because you think them possessed of such a law, and hold them to be men bound to live according to it? But do you not see that in so judging, you are paying the highest possible tribute to their religion? To the degree that you condemn the men, you praise their law; in holding that they ought to have been the best in living, you acknowledge that their religion was the best. The standard you apply to Israel, Israel supplied to you, but in falling below it, what did Israel confess but that his standard was not of himself, but of his God?

III

1. We have seen, then, the new theistic or religious idea and the people in themselves and in their mutual relations. We must now proceed a step further. Remember that the determinative thing in religion

is the character of God. Well, we have got a God with a moral character, but have made no attempt at an analysis of its moral elements. These, when we first find the idea, are few and simple, but its character becomes in process of time ethically sublimer, purer, richer. Here, the first thing necessary is to see how, even in its simplest form, the new idea affected the organization of society and the regulation of life. These two,—the thought of the divine and the thought of the human,—are related as ideal and reality, as design and structure; and so we can test by history the action of the divine idea in human society and life. For here it acted according to a law common in all religions, the highest idea is distinguished from all others by its being the force which causes the society to crystallize or become an organism. In order that we may perceive what this means, let me ask—Suppose you conceive God as force, or soul, or energy, without morality or moral character, then how would you conceive human life and human society? A man may say, "I believe in force, and I believe in necessity, yet I am a moral man, and hold a moral theory of life." But see, there is no logic like the logic of fact. There is no law of reason so inevitable as the law that fulfils itself in historical movement. We are able to see when we turn to history the regulative and organizing power of a highest conception which is void of moral qualities and acts by necessity, working on the most stupendous scale. Let us look at India. What has been the great organizing power of society there? The notion of Brahma. That name represents a conception as nearly as possible parallel to Mr. Herbert Spencer's "persistent force." Brahma is an ever-acting indestructible energy. From him proceed by necessity all the forms, varieties, forces of life. What men call the soul, comes to be by necessary law, revolves through innumerable cycles, remaining in each and in all the same as to essence, changing only its form. The human person is a transitory shape or vehicle, which incarnates and carries the soul—which is an entity, or atom, or invisible force that circles from form of being to form of being, until its cycle of multitudinous changes being complete it is absorbed into Brahma. The life that now is, which is determined by lives that have been, determines in its turn lives to be; each life is but one new link in the chain forged by Brahma, who sits at the source of Being, a necessitated creator, and waits at its end, an unconscious goal. While individual life is so conceived, what of the social, the collective? Man's place here is determined by that awful, inevitable force which binds his various forms of existence together. Now, as it depended on whence the soul or person had first proceeded, from the head or from the feet of Brahma, whether the man was to be high caste or low caste, so the whole social system was a system that expressed in an organized form the operation of an unmoral cause. There was no moral basis of society, only one of prerogative and privilege ;

and so, as a necessary result, to break caste was to break the highest law. There was no sin like the sin of infidelity to caste, the worst apostasy was for a high caste to become an outcast, the last presumption for a low caste to attempt to enter a higher. And so India represents a society organized on the principle of a creative force without moral idea or quality, and shows on the most stupendous scale that from such a conception, the only possible result is tyranny, or a life governed by an unmoral necessity. If the cause of man and society be not moral, neither the man nor the society can recognize moral law as their regulative principle, and where moral law is not so recognized, force,—either physical, civil, or sacerdotal,—is the only alternative.

2. Let us turn now to the regulative and organizing action of the Old Testament idea of God. This we have to observe in its most rudimentary form in the Mosaic Society. And here let me ask you to note what I may call its extraordinary Secularism. By that term I mean to indicate the place given to time, and to realizing in time the order that should express the mind and will of God. It is simply a matter of exegetical and historical fact, that of all religions in antiquity, the Mosaic laid least stress upon the future state, or life to come. This, of course, relates to its earliest stage. But it is here that the value of the idea as a new basis for society can best be seen. There was a very great and learned book written last century by a most belligerent divine, a mighty

man of controversial valour—Bishop Warburton. Its name was *The Divine Legation of Moses*, and its purpose was to prove what has been well held to be a paradox, this, namely, that the Hebrew or Mosaic religion was, by its not appealing to the sanctions of the future, proved to be of divine institution, and altogether miraculous in character. All other religions, it was argued, maintained their authority, by invoking the sanctions of another world. To this, the Hebrew was an exception, and since it ruled without help from the future, it could only have come to be by the direct action of God, and have continued authoritative by His immediate and constant guidance and superintendence. Now, I do not mean to endorse that opinion, or even so much of it as relates to the absence of the sanction drawn from the future life, but this I mean to do, to say that emphasis was in the Mosaic state laid on the present, on time, on the construction of such a state in the world that now is as should be altogether in harmony with the will of God. The men who were called to constitute that state, were not invited to do so in view of rewards and punishments that were to follow in another life. They were not able to glory in the inequalities of this life as certain to be redressed by the rewards of the life to come. They were not persuaded to neglect the transient present because of an imperishable future, but they were told to build up where they stood, as living men, a city that was in its laws, in its character, its work, its ideal, to be a city of God, a state constituted and constructed according to the divine plan. And this was to be done because God, who created the world, so commanded. And as he was moral, the laws that were at the root of the whole were moral laws, enforced reverence to God, dependence upon Him, worship that was moral obedience, truthfulness, honesty, chastity, neighbourliness, filial devotion, and love.

Two points here call for notice:—first, the independence of the Mosaic ideal of the future proves the absolute independence of the Mosaic religion of Egypt. The Egyptian religion was a religion of the future, absolutely and altogether concerned about man's happiness there. The Mosaic was the religion of the present, making men work in it for God and His purposes, for man and his good. And, secondly, this religion, as giving a moral law alike to the individual and to society was an absolutely new thing. Not only did it directly concern the present, but the idea, as applied to the governance and organization of life, made God the supreme law-giver, while His supreme law was moral. He founded the state, He gave the law. He called the state into being for His purposes, and to do so was to give it a sublimity that no other ancient state had, a universality not of fact, but of idea, that made it without a parallel or a peer amid all the ancient states and empires. Where the fundamental laws of a people are moral, and are the laws of a moral Deity, the tyrannies of despotism and conquest or force are at an end.

IV

1. But now we shall the better study the action of this great creative idea when we place it in relation to the notion of man. This must correspond to the notion of God. The one is the counterpart and mirror of the other. Now the Mosaic religion, as it was the first that had the idea of a moral Deity, was also the first that had the notion of man as a moral, free, conscious individual, with rights no man could take from him, and with duties no man could fulfil for him. The full significance of this, especially as regards its social and political action, will become apparent if you note this—that the great notion in all the ancient Empires was, the king or the priest owns the people. The idea of man as a conscious, rational, moral individual, of worth for his own sake, of equal dignity before his Maker, did not exist in antiquity till it came into being through Israel. Do you think I mis-state the matter? Let us see the fact. Did you ever look at the great pyramids of Egypt and ask, why or how they came to be? Millions of nameless men died to create for two or three almost unknown kings a tomb. Look at the largest :—one hundred thousand men are said to have worked by forced labour every day at its building, and it took twenty years to build. A hundred thousand men driven by force through twenty years

to unpaid labour, and all to build a tomb for a king!
Imagine every able-bodied man in a city as large as
Manchester or Liverpool, forced for twenty years to
work without pay for the vanity of one man, and you
have a single illustration of the value of man and his
work as the remoter antiquity understood it. Do
not let this surprise you. Take some of the hymns
of ancient Egypt, which of late years have been re-
covered, and you will find the king praised as god,
extolled as divine, all divine qualities being attributed
to him. Pass from the valley of the Nile to the valley
of the Euphrates, and ask what do you find there?
The king is the master of men, he can muster his
thousands by will, by will he can throw his thousands
away, and it is his concern if the men are lost; the
loss is his, not theirs. No man has worth, save to the
king and for his ends. No man is valued as a person,
or as a man. The idea of manhood, as anything
real or possible, does not as yet exist. Go still
further east, to India, and what do you find? As a
man acts to the priest, the Brahman, so his place in
this life and the life to come is determined. Whatever maintains the purity of caste is right, whatever
interferes with it is wrong, and life is everywhere
under a shadow because without the dignifying
presence of the moral ideal. But when the Mosaic
state came into being, what did it bring with it? A
new notion of man, a higher conception of manhood. It had no king, God was King, every man of
the people was precious in God's sight, each had an

equal worth, all had equal duties and equal rights. The idea of the rights of man and the correlative idea of his duties, were created by the religion that gave the moral idea of God. In no ancient state was man more dignified, was life so valued. To touch it was to touch what God made and protected. The very sovereign was good only as he did God's will, and his last sin was to oppress the people he had received from God.

2. But we have not only to consider the idea of man, we have to see man built into a state. Now the basis of the state is a moral one. And it is moral because it is the will, the expressed will of the moral Deity. God is to be honoured as the One God. He is to be revered. Man is to remain pure, to be no adulterer, to speak the truth, not to covet, not to kill, not to steal. All duty laid down by God is law to be fulfilled by man. Now, I have already said that the gods of the ancients were, as a rule, unmoral or immoral, that as a consequence religion was no friend to morality, was often most lustful and impure. But now, note, that in and under and because of Moses came the idea that to serve God you must do your duty by man, must be obedient and faithful in the simplest daily things. Now, I do not intend to defend the Mosaic law—which is here taken to mean no more than those ten Commandments which are the heart of all the Levitical legislation—as a perfect law for all time, or to say that it contains all morality. It was impossible that

the earliest form of the Hebrew religion could be as perfect as the latest, but it had as a germ all the capabilities of growth and expansion needed for ultimate perfection. And this I further say, that from this moment moral life at once in the state and in the man is based and built on this great ethical conception of God, and God's will, as a moral will, becomes the basis of human society.

Now, we have to observe a further consequence, the state became God's. This, too, was a new idea. In every other ancient state, in Greece, in India, in Assyria, in Egypt, the state owned the gods. They were the state's. The state possessed the religion, and the men who belonged to it must be of its faith. If a man questioned the gods, he questioned the law, was guilty of treason in its most offensive form, and so the state put him to death. To question the law of the state in matters of religion was so much a crime in the eyes of the heathen that persecution seemed a natural and obvious necessity. It was indeed the coming of heathen ideas into the Christian religion that made freedom of thought anywhere in any Christian land a crime. You will see then that the notion of the ancient world was by the Hebrews here reversed ; the state did not own God, He owned it, founded it, and founded it in order that His will, a moral will, might be done within it. That is the fundamental social conception of the most ancient Hebrew legislation, and it is therefore moral while social, and moral and social because religious — the Moral Deity is the basis of society, and He proclaims, defines, and enforces the law regulative of life, both individual and collective.

V

1. But the law could not be moral without becoming much more, and so it had to become social, economical, and religious as well. And this in the course of the centuries it became, progressively more and more. Yet the influence of the moral centre and basis never ceased to extend to the circumference and summit. As to these wider aspects I cannot speak in detail, but will simply note three points. First, of the law in relation to Nature. There never was a saner law than the Mosaic. It loved Nature, could not bear to see the fields impoverished, and decreed that no man should be allowed to injure either his posterity, or his neighbours, or the land on which they lived, by impoverishing its fields. Nor could it bear to see the human form mutilated, and so it declared that only the unblemished was beautiful in the sight of God, and fit to do Him public and sacred service. It did not love to harass or burden the dumb creation; the ox that trod out the corn was not to be muzzled. The young tender tree was protected, and was not to be unduly taxed to yield abundance. The law was thus full of a great sense of the good of nature, a great sense

of the glory within humanity, and of the large and lovely harmony without.

Secondly, the law in relation to man. There never was so careful a law about what we call sanitation. It cared for the cleanliness of the body. It feared infection, and separated those with infectious diseases from the great multitude, declaring them unclean. Its laws of ceremonial uncleanness had great health in them—a real human sanity. Then, though it knew slavery, as all the ancient world did, the slavery it knew was of the gentlest, the most generous kind. Every man taken as a slave could, in the sabbatic year, regain his freedom, go forth into the world a free man. Its laws, too, concerning the wealth of man, were noble laws. They made property sacred, yet did not allow its accumulation in a few hands, or in one, but sought to secure its fair and equal distribution. Every Jubilee year the land was redistributed; the old families that had lost it might again possess their inheritance. And so if by misfortune, or by crime, a man had lost his estate, he had a chance given to him to redeem himself and his place in the community, to go back into his old and better order. Capital, also, was carefully guarded, that it should not become an immense and oppressive power in the hands of the rich, to make them extortionate over the poor. We may indeed, without fear of contradiction, affirm that the Jewish law is the justest law to the poor yet framed, to the man that toiled, to the man prepared honestly by sweat of brow and labour of hand to earn his bread. Let us do it justice. I ask for it from you only justice, but justice I do ask ; for that is only a just demand. Where the idea of a moral God and a free, responsible man came in and held possession of the people, there, applied to the questions of industry and economics, emerged a law that secured, as far as law can secure such things, the equitable distribution of wealth, and the highest degree of individual wellbeing.

But, thirdly, we have to note a characteristic peculiarity in the laws relating to God and His service. Among the surrounding states of antiquity the Mosaic state stood distinguished for one thing, the absence of human sacrifice, a matter most significant as to the character of God, as to His way of educating and teaching man. Human sacrifice was one of the commonest and most horrible rites of the ancient religions. And it was one of the hardest things to bring the Jewish people out of the common and coarser into the rarer and kindlier service. Remember that question which the prophet represents the king as asking : " How shall I come before the Lord, and bow myself before the most high God ? Shall I give the fruit of my body for the sin of my soul ? " That was a common question in the ancient religions. But in its answer Israel stood alone and pre-eminent :—" He hath showed thee, O man, what is good. And what doth the Lord require of thee, but to do justly, to love mercy, and to walk humbly with thy God?" The answer is significant alike of the new dignity and worth of man, and of the new and noble tenderness in the character of his God.

But you may say, "See how many of the laws are imperfect and severe, nay, even cruel. Take, for example, the law against witchcraft. 'Thou shalt not suffer a witch to live.' Had not that law to do with the burnings for witchcraft in the sixteenth, seventeenth, and eighteenth centuries? And how can you defend the religion against the charge of burning people for an impossible crime?" Now there are here two questions, one as to the law, and another as to its interpretation or application in later history. "Thou shalt not suffer a witch to live," must be looked at through the eyes of that time, in the spirit of a historical student, asking the meaning of a religion, and what witchcraft signified to it. It did not mean an old woman addicted to black arts, who burnt before the fire the image of a man who was thought to decay as the image melted. It meant the presence and power of the religions lying around. It stood in necessary alliance with them, and in necessary antithesis to the fundamental idea of a moral religion, realized in a moral life. And it was a simple necessity if the religion of Israel was to remain and not be superseded by the cruel and lascivious religion of Phœnicia, that the witch who was, as it were, the very prophet and priestess of Phœnicia, and the worst elements in heathenism, should not be suffered to live in Israel. The other question, as to its interpretation and application two or three centuries ago, is another matter altogether, and for it the men of that time are alone responsible. They did two things—they misunderstood the purport and function of the Mosaic law, and they forgot the relation in which it stood to the law of Christ. It was only preparatory, provisional, intended for a time long past, and passing with the time for which it was intended. Any man who scientifically looks at the matter, sees that the law of Moses, or the ideal of the Mosaic state, was not universal and permanent, intended for all time. Men have thought that it was, as perhaps Calvin, when he founded his Theocracy at Geneva, and the Puritans, when they founded their Church-State over in New England. The mistakes of these men are to be judged, like all other mistakes of historical interpretation, as reflecting on the men, and not on the law they misunderstood. Then, for the further point, come to the moment when Christ declared the true yet simple relation in which the transitory and permanent in the old law stood to Himself. It had been said, "An eye for an eye, and a tooth for a tooth, but I say unto you, that ye resist not evil." Here was a law written and formulated as Mosaic, but it was a law designed and fitted only for an imperfect state, intended, therefore, to be repealed and cancelled in a state higher and more perfect. And this single is an illustrative case. Do not judge a provisional as if it were a permanent law, a law for a people like the Hebrews as if it had been the ultimate code of the Christian Church. The moral elements in Moses abide, the ceremonial and occasional have passed and perished.

2. We have as yet discussed but a very small part of a very great subject; and time will allow us to discuss no more. All that has been attempted has been to bring out the distinctive Hebrew conception of God as the source and basis of the distinctive Hebrew state. We must end; yet I feel as if I had not brought you even within sight of the boundless riches of the marvellous book which we call the Scriptures of the Old Testament. Here, indeed, one feels the pathos of standing on the narrow shore, and looking over the boundless, unexplored, mysterious ocean. Beside us a prosaic disputant may stand and say, "What see you but a barren expanse of water, vexed by angry winds?" But let our answer be: "Man, be silent; we are looking over the mighty pathway of the peoples, and we see it thronged with argosies hastening to distribute their unsearchable wealth among all kindreds of the world." It is not possible to describe this wealth, but let me in a hurried sentence or two indicate its kind and extent. Well, then, no literature of antiquity is possessed with so deep a love of the poor, speaks so strong and generous words concerning them, surrounds them with so much dignity and so many rights as this Old Testament. I know what I say, and I say

what no man who knows antiquity can contradict. Without the Bible labour would be without its noblest vindicator, without the one ancient witness that testified in behalf of its honour and its claims. There is no book that so denounces the king who dares to oppress, or the priest who dares to deceive the poor, that so praises the man who does justice and loves mercy. To help the poor is to please God, to wrong them is to provoke His wrath. The ideal king is one who "Shall govern thy people with righteousness, and thy poor with judgment." "He shall save the children of the needy, and shall break in pieces the oppressor." " He shall deliver the poor, and him that hath no helper." " He shall redeem their soul from deceit and violence, and precious shall their blood be in his sight." Connected herewith is its love of the weak and defenceless, the way it seeks to honour and guard the woman and child. Do you know how Roman law dealt with the father? It invested him within his family with absolute power, over against him the wife and child could not be said to possess any rights; and the Roman law is the finest blossom of the Roman spirit, and in the field of civil legislation of all antiquity. But in the Old Testament the great preachers who speak in the name of God will allow no such absolute power to man ; not right, but duty is in proportion to strength; the greater the weakness, the greater the claim on the resourceful and the strong. "Children are an heritage of the Lord," to be dealt with as riches held in trust for Him. The man He most approves is the one who "judges the fatherless and pleads for the widow." Then there is no book so full of the love of honesty, the praise of justice between man and man. It hates "the false balance," the lying tongue, the over-reaching spirit. It commends alike the generous master and the faithful servant. In a word, its ideal of life—industrial, domestic, civil, commercial—is the highest, purest, sublimest, known to the ancient world, for it is an ideal that struggles towards the creation of righteousness in all persons and in all relations.

But why attempt to sketch in hasty words the meaning and wealth of this marvellous literature? Let me simply urge you to read it anew, with open eye and clear vision. Look at its proverbs, so laden with moral wisdom, so possessed with the belief that true goodness is best prudence, and obedience to God the condition of all good. Look at its Psalms; what wonderful poetry is there! It has no parallel or peer. For thousands of years these Psalms have been sung, and men sing them still, feeling as if they were the most modern, the most living of all religious songs. They have been translated out of their primitive Hebrew speech into almost all our human tongues, and have become, as it were, the universal language in which man can tell his joy or sorrow, his contrition or exultation, to God. Then, look at its attitude to the profoundest of all the problems that can vex the human spirit, the problem of the good man suffering in an evil world! That was the problem of Job and the second part of Isaiah; in the one the perfect man is the man who suffers most, in the other the servant of God, his anointed, in whom his soul delighted, is the Man of Sorrows, and acquainted with grief. The perfect man and servant suffers that he may redeem; his holiness and our sin are the twin causes of his sorrow, but as the sorrow of the holy it can save the man who has sinned. His suffering is the redemption of his kind. Then, think, with all its sense of evil and sorrow it never lost hope, but found in the presence of wrong only a deeper need for faith in a righteous God, new ground for confidence in a reign that would right all. And so we see those marvellous prophets, turning from a time of impotence and evil, when the little handful of their people, beset, harassed, hunted, broken, could not realize their own imperfect vision of the prophetic ideal, look forward and anticipate the true golden age when peace and joy among nations, wealth and perfect manhood among men, should everywhere prevail. The fulfilment of their vision tarries, but their God reigns, and it will surely come!

III

THE PLACE AND SIGNIFICANCE OF THE NEW TESTAMENT IN RELIGION

THE fundamental idea of the previous lecture was this—The religion of Israel was an altogether new order of religion, and it was this by virtue of its conception or thought of God and His law. By means of these it laid the basis for a new notion of man, a new type of society, a new structure or order of humanity. So long as men believe in a multitude of gods, they will never believe in the unity of man; so long as they believe in a deity without moral character, they will never live under what they feel to be a common moral law. Might will be right. Their world will be the strong man's world, where the weakest goes to the wall, and the poor, unpitied, live or die to please the rich.

I

1. Now, the change that has made our idea of man and society so unlike the ancient, is a change that begins with the notion of God and His law that came

through Moses. That is a simple matter of historic fact and certainty. No code of antiquity possessed, in anything like the same degree, so exalted a notion of man, of the rights of man, of the dignity of man's labour, of his duties, of his moral worth and relations, of his claim to reap and to possess the harvest of profit, or of plenty, his own hands had sowed. It was not the priest's, or the king's law, it was God's. In that lay the secret of its power, the source of the great dignity it gave to man. Make the law the king's or the priest's, make king or priest own the people, and you have as an inevitable result despotism, oppression, wrong, sacrifice of the weak to the strong. Make the law and the people God's, and you have as an inevitable result, the equality of all men before God, and, once that is clearly and fully understood, the equal freedom and the equal rights of all men. The law which came through Moses was, to the people as a whole, the most generous, the most righteous law of antiquity, reposing as it did on the humanest of all the ancient conceptions of God.

Now, I wish to restate and re-emphasize this central and fundamental idea, or principle. Whatever men may say, it is incontestable, a simple fact which history has verified. You will never build a society or a state, ordered, free, righteous, unless you build it on a great moral belief, and the greatest of all moral beliefs is the belief in a moral Deity ; for that makes the source, the laws, the method, the course, the end of life, all alike moral. A society built up from the foundation consistently according to that notion, would be a perfect society, but to a perfect society you need not only a great theoretic principle, you need perfect persons, equal in their perfection to the theoretic belief they hold. But the function of great beliefs is not to find perfect men, but to make them, to take the poor material it gets, and out of it to build up nobler characters and nobler men. To take the individual, the isolated men and acts of a given race, or a given people, and make the system bear the blame of their imperfections, is to act, perhaps, in the spirit of controversy, but not in the spirit of science, which seeks to discover the action, through persons or peoples, of great beliefs on man, and in this action to see their character and quality revealed. Now I am able to say, as another simple and incontrovertible fact, of all ancient literatures, of all ancient writings possessed by man, the writings with the largest sense of humanity, the greatest sense of the rights of the individual, the noblest conception of labour and its reward, of society and its functions, are the writings of the Hebrews. Nowhere is the king so reproved, nowhere is the priest so reproached, when either dares to forget his supreme obedience to God, or his supreme duty to man. If either dares so to forget, the prophet stands forward, and says, "Bring no more vain oblations: incense is abomination unto God; your new moons and your appointed feasts His soul hateth. Wash you, make you clean; put away the evil of your doings from before His eyes ; cease to do evil ; learn to do well ; seek judgment, relieve the oppressed, judge the fatherless, plead for the widow."

Now let me ask you as open-minded men to consider this simple question ; since every ancient empire, as the pyramids of Egypt and the records of Babylonia show us, despised the common people, forced them to labour as if they had no claim or right to their own strength and the profits of their own skill, and threw away their lives as if they had no personal worth—Why is it otherwise with us ? Modern Oriental empires, where the ancient basis of society still in a measure survives, have the old contempt of man and life. China will see a thousand men perish with less concern than we would see a score. Before we went to India life was squandered as if it were a worthless thing ; our care for life in India has within this century caused so extraordinary an increase of the population as to bring upon us the gravest of all economical questions—How deal with a people whose increase threatens to outrun the means of subsistence ? Why, then, do we so value life ? Why do we so value man that we seek to secure to every one the reward of his own labour ? Why do we so hate the pestilence or the famine, the war or the accident, which comes to destroy noble and valued being ? History supplies the answer, the facts which cannot be disputed, and they say that the right to your own labour, to your own manhood, to your very personal freedom, in a word, the ideas that make men of you, run back into the belief in God and God's law that came through Moses.

Let us abide by the facts ; do not let any man divert you from them and what they teach. Do not let a sneer at a Hebrew patriarch or king by a man too ill-informed and prejudiced to understand him, and the times in which he lived, lead you away from the real point at issue—Why is man and his labour, why are the common people and their rights, so differently esteemed and valued now from what they were in the ancient world ? And comparative science, working with the historical material, finds only one answer—these ideas rose in connection with the religion of Israel, and have their primary source and basis in the great beliefs it created and supplied. Yet it was only provisional, imperfect, a mere prophecy of a more perfect method, of a nobler order and a larger faith. Without the preparatory, the final and perfect could not have been ; without the perfect, the preparatory had been but a promise, a blossom that had never rounded and ripened into fruit.

2. We come now, then, to the New Testament and its significance for our question. In dealing with it we must not change our standpoint or our method. We must apply the same principles ; we must look at all matters under the same lights as heretofore. Now, while the religion of the Old Testament aimed at creating a state or organizing a people on the basis of the belief in the one personal and moral

Deity, and of obedience to His law, we may describe the religion of the New Testament as a method for creating and constituting a new humanity, and this new mankind it seeks to create and constitute by its idea of God, and what that idea contains and makes manifest. It is not, observe, a religion of anxious individualism, concerned about nothing except saving isolated souls; careful only to make men contented in life, peaceful in death, and happy in eternity. It may accomplish these, but they are only means, not ends. In its essence it is a mighty plan, splendid in its design and in its efficiency, for the construction, from the base upwards, of a humanity or a society that shall, in all its parts, through all its members, in all its relations, express or articulate the righteous will of God. It is thus an ideal for the whole of humanity, and a great method for its realization. It is at this point that it stands at once related to the religion of Israel and distinguished from it; what Israel tried to do for a people, the New Testament came to do for mankind. What existed as particular and provisional in the old, exists as general and permanent in the new.

Here, again, the great constitutive factor, changing and regulating the individual, building up and organizing the society, is the conception of God. And the place He occupies, as well as the way in which He is conceived, makes a generic difference between the Christian and other religions. Varro, an old and most learned Roman, said, " In order that gods may be established, states must first exist." That was the pagan idea, the state owned the god, and the god had no power or authority outside its own state. In perfect harmony with this notion the emperor or king was deified in a way that greatly astonishes the men of to-day. Suppose the people of England were to call their Queen goddess; or suppose the people of Russia, dark and benighted as they may seem, were to call a man, whose moral character was like the late Emperor's, god, what would you think of them? Yet in the days of Christ and His apostles, the high bloom-time of the Roman empire, men like Nero, who could fiddle while Rome burned; men like Caligula, who drank, feasted, and committed crime of the worst imaginable sorts, were called divine, and they received honour and worship as gods. Yet, strange as all this may seem, it was logical, it grew out of the idea that the state was greater than the religion, and established the gods; they did not own but were owned by the state, it was their factor, they were not its. And as the state was thus more divine and comprehensive than the religion, the person who symbolized its authority, its unity, and being, could be fitly termed *divus* or even *deus*. Now why would the use of the term goddess to queen or god to emperor seem to us so profane? Is it not because there has passed into our blood, into the very marrow, as it were, of our spirit and mind, a conception of deity that makes these old conceptions unutterably degrading? But does not this very elevation of our conception of the divine measure the influence of Christianity? It has so exalted every man's idea of God as to make the ancient idea abhorrent where it is not unintelligible.

II

1. Now if we are to understand the significance of the New Testament for our discussion, we must come to it with open spirit, and look at its idea of religion as embodied in its great Personality. In other words, we must seek to understand its idea through Christ. Now His life was one of very remarkable simplicity, and one of still more remarkable significance. It was altogether, from the religious point of view, unlike the ideal that had become traditional in Israel. For religions may grow, but they may also decay, and the distance between the vision and thought of an Isaiah, and the ideal and embodiment of a priest or a scribe or a pharisee in the day of Christ is almost immeasurable. The traditional ideal in Christ's day, the period of decadence, was twofold, there was the priest's, and there was the scribe's. The priest's idea was—the temple, the worship, the priesthood are the religion. God dwells in the temple; He is approached through His priesthood, He is appeased by their sacrifices, and the most pious man is the man who most often visits the temple, uses the priesthood, offers the costliest and greatest oblations. The idea of the scribe was different, yet akin. It was an

ideal of forms, full of fasts and holy days, formulas and prayers, positions and phylacteries, reading of Scriptures and general performance of things by rule. In short, it was men living by rote, according to the fashion of the fathers or the times. The priests said, "No man can please God, unless he worships in a consecrated place, employs authorized persons, uses the proper and catholic means." The scribe said, "No man can worship God, unless he stands by tradition and follows what it prescribes." Worthy men they were, no doubt, honest after their lights, scrupulous, obedient to every jot and tittle of the law, forgetful only of one thing—that the law of God was infinitely greater than their thoughts. Their ideals, I have said, were akin, and their kinship stands expressed here :—they made scrupulous men, men of most rigid conscientiousness, who would have gone to prison or the stake for a rite or a privilege, but they never yet made magnanimous men, who would have died for humanity.

These, then, were the traditional ideals, religion as materialized and depraved by priest and scribe. Now Christ's ideal was essentially different. To them He was utterly unintelligible, a person not to be understood. He lived away in Galilee, remote from the city of the religion, and so at first came but seldom into conflict with the priests. They could not understand a person pre-eminent in religion, who would not, and did not, frequent the temple according to rule and routine and season, and use the sacrifices.

With the scribes, again, He was in ceaseless collision about their weightiest matters of the law, their solemn days, their fasts, their feasts, their periods of prayer, their tithing mint, anise, and cummin, about the formal ways, all so little, yet all so burdensome, in which they thought to do religious work. When He went through the fields on the Sabbath, and His disciples plucked the ears of corn, they thought and spoke as if He had broken the whole law of God; and when He opposed to their "Thus saith the fathers, or thus saith tradition," His own authority as Son of Man and Lord of the Sabbath, they only thought Him guilty of the deeper profanity and even the worst blasphemy. He was too elevated to be understood of them, and so was misunderstood in the gravest degree, and to the most disastrous results. Not to fulfil their ideal was to be worthy of the cross.

2. But while his ideal stood in opposition to theirs, see how noble it looks by the contrast. He was the Son of Man and the Son of God, and He seemed to lie as it were embosomed in the Father's arms, feeling as if round His path and about His soul, in darkest hour, in supremest moment, the divine hands watched to guide and to bless. He felt at all times at home with God; He lived in God, God lived in Him; men felt in His presence as in the presence of the Father, because in the presence of the only begotten Son. And, note, when He became religiously active, what He did, and where He was found. Not in the temple, but in the highway, where disease was to be

cured ; in the home where wisdom was to be taught ; on the sea, and by the shore, where men were prepared to listen ; at the receipt of custom, or in the haunts of the outcast, where men were waiting to be saved ; there, where He could best bring to lost men the great message of life, there was He found. And, high though He seemed, He gave to no man the sense that He condescended ; great though His acts were, His condescension was never conscious. What He did was through the gracious and sweet compulsion of a true and holy love. What God is among His worlds, Christ was among men. He was the minister of God for good to man, come to give His life a ransom for many. He was the great Helper of the forlorn, the Saviour who seized and uplifted the lowly, and carried on His own weary shoulders the burden of guilt that crushed men to the earth. And what feeling did He give them? A new strange feeling, making the men who were guilty feel a passion for good ; He changed the sense of sin in the outcast into the sense of sonship, the being beloved of the Father and the Son. He loved love into being, and commanded by the love He begot. And so the ideal of religion He realized was altogether new ; it needed for its being no priest, no scribe, no temple, save the temple of a pure and true spirit and the presence of a loving God, no order consecrated and set apart to sacerdotal functions and ceremonious duties, but only the consecrated spirit of the child face to face with the Father. Where love is, the intrusion of a priest is an impertinence, a dark shade that sheds coldness into the spirit. And where would it have been so impertinent as on the heart and in the Spirit of Him who, as Son of Man and Son of God, sorrowed in Gethsemane, and died on the cross?

3. As His religion was in deed, so in word. What He lived He taught. What He taught He lived. Many remarkable elements about that teaching might here be summarized and described, strange, remarkable elements, too. Here is the Founder of a religion. Then what does He do? In the life He lives He never does a priestly act, or gives Himself a priestly name, never assumes towards man the attitude, or manifests the temper, or falls into the tone of the conventional priest. More, He founds His society, and He does not name any man He calls to office within it priest, appoints no man to do any priestly act, institutes no official priesthood, simply and purely makes them apostles, or disciples, or prophets, men who learned, and men who taught, or who learned that they might teach. When He wishes to impress great duties upon men, how does He do it? By parable. And when He uses the parable to enforce the highest duty man owes to man, where does He get His example, His impersonation of love? In the priest and the Levite? Nay, in the man they held to be unclean and an outcast, the Samaritan. When He wishes to express duty to God, the true idea of prayer, where does He get His type? Not from the man who has his formula and his book, his regular fasts and his legal tithes, but in the

publican, who prays out of his stricken conscience, "God be merciful to me, a sinner." And here the Pharisee, the man of forms, stands in the background to make the picture more distinct. And when He wishes to find the qualities He most praises, where does He find them? Not in the old conventional ideal, but in the pure in heart, the peacemaker, the lover of righteousness, the sufferer, the man that mourns. They are the blessed, and if He wishes to describe the supreme law of God, He finds it in two things, love to God in heaven, love to man on earth. On these hang all the law and the prophets. Nay, more, He so combines these, as to make each involve the other, as if He meant to say—where perfect love is to God, there will perfect love be to man, and where love to man, there all the duties God requires will be fulfilled.

But observe; the maxims, ethical and moral, do not stand alone. They are part of a vast and immense system. They are built on a great foundation. They rise out of the conception of God, and His relation to man. Then, note, He does not mean the people He calls to remain individuals, shut off from each other; He associates them in a great kingdom. That kingdom is called of heaven; which means, it is not like the kingdoms of earth, created by physical power, planted by passion or pride—that were despotism; but it came from above down into man, and must be received freely to be received at all. Then He says, it is a kingdom of God. That means, it does not come from the act of might or tyranny or deception, the ambition of some great man, planted on the throne of empire; it was God's, meant to be realized in conscience, to show the authority of God over the man. The people drawn into that kingdom, are drawn into it by the truth, that is, its citizens are obedient to the truth by belief of the truth. The men that compose it are men that must not seek to extend it by sword or persecution, by civil law or military power. It is a kingdom of the truth, standing, extending, reigning, only through the truth and the agencies it employs. Within that kingdom, which has no visible form and can know no limits of time and place, the faithful and holy men of all ages and races are gathered, and, all unconsciously to themselves, are engaged in a common labour, working together with God through His Son in building up a new humanity, where, instead of the old despotism of force, the new force of divine love shall reign supreme. That kingdom is an eternal ideal ever in process of realization, never to be perfectly realized. Yet it is all the mightier because it is so ideal, because it means that our most perfect state is but the shadow of the most perfect possible. In the mind of God there lies a pattern according to which the new creation is made, and that pattern is the kingdom which Jesus instituted, and which His people constitute. Within it truth reigns, law rules, and obedience is realized. It has come, yet it is only coming; when a man has entered it, he is a citizen of God's city. Once it is completely realized on earth, the will of God will be done here as in heaven.

III

But hitherto we have been concerned only with the personal religion and ideal of Jesus: yet these implied and reposed on certain great truths; were, indeed, just their articulation or expression in the region of reality and life. Now we must descend to these truths themselves; it is only through them that we can understand the person and work of Christ. I am not going to ask you to discuss the high theological doctrine of the Godhead, but only to consider this—a person and work like Christ's is a superstructure, cannot stand on nothing, can be there and abide only provided it be built on a foundation of reality and truth. Now it is not possible either to state or discuss what we may call these sub-structural truths; but I wish you to look at those aspects of them that bear on the idea of religion, and those questions concerning its action in history that are meanwhile before us. The analysis and presentation of Christ's personal ideal of religion has prepared us for this new discussion.

1. We shall best begin by returning to our fundamental principle; the idea of the divine is the determinative idea. A religion always is as its deity is, or, in other words, a man is made by his thought of God or what stands in its place. There

is no surer measure of a people's progress than its successive conceptions of the Being it worships. The deities of a rude age become little better than the devils of an age more refined. The evil power the savage propitiates, the sage despises or disbelieves. If, therefore, a religion stands rooted in a depraved or narrow notion of God, it can never become or continue to be the religion of a civilized and progressive people. The gods the Homeric Greeks believed in were abhorrent to the pious men of the Socratic schools, to the exalted mind of Xenophanes, to the devout spirit of Plato, and the subtle intellect of Aristotle. Yet their ideas are to us hardly more real than the Homeric. The destiny of Æschylos, inevitable, merciless, moving resistless to punish unconscious as well as conscious sin, is a dread power from which the heart of the world shrinks, a power it could never in its soul worship, but only so soon as it had courage repudiate or deny. The God of Islam, solitary, severe, stern, inducing man to obey by motives that debase, depraving woman, hating the infidel, handing him over to the exterminating sword, is a fit deity for wild Arabs, or fierce Turks, but no god for civilized and free man. Even the God certain ancient Jews conceived, jealous, angry, vengeful, taking pleasure in seeing the little ones of the heathen dashed against the stones, is not a being that, so conceived, can remain the divine sovereign of man. The ultimate and absolute God of man must bear on him the mark of no age, no place, no race, must stand over all like His own heaven, be like it luminous, serene, unsullied, receiving the foul breath of earth only to purify it, its fragrance only to send it back in holy and gentle influences.

And what is the Christian idea? That God is the Father, the Common Father of man, universal, everlasting in His love. He hates no child, misconduct does not create dislike. Love was the end for which He made the world, for which He made every human soul. His glory is to diffuse happiness, to fill up the silent places of the universe with voices that speak out of glad hearts. As a Father He cannot but be Sovereign, for the patriarch is the absolute king. As Sovereign He cannot but enforce order, for only thus can the end which is love be obtained. But He is first Father, then Sovereign, anxious to assert His authority, not for the sake of the law, but to save His child. Because He made man for love He cannot bear man to be lost, rather than see the loss fall on man He will suffer sacrifice; sacrifice to Him will become joy when it restores the ruined, but loss to man will be absolute, for losing himself he loses all. So the great Father loves man in spite of his sin, in the midst of his guilt, loves that He may save, and even should He fail in saving, He does not cease to love. In the place we call hell eternal love as really is as in the place we call heaven, though in the one case it is the complacency or pleasure in the holy and the happy which seems like the brightness of everlasting sunshine or the glad music of waves that break into perennial laughter, but in the other it is the compassion or pity for the bad and the miserable which seems like a face shaded with everlasting regret, or the muffled weeping of a sorrow too deep to be heard. That grand thought of a God who is the eternal and universal Father, all the more regal a Sovereign that He is so absolutely Father, can never fail to touch the heart of the man who understands it, be he savage or sage.

2. But this extraordinary elevation of the idea of God could not stand alone, it affected every region of thought and feeling. The first thing it touched and ennobled was the idea of man. The more divinely men thought of God, the more highly they thought of man. Into the new conception of God all the sublime and strong elements of the old had been received, but exalted and softened, made at once majestic and gracious. Men at a given stage of culture understand severity better than gentleness ; and so the severer aspect of God came first, because the men Moses led out of Egypt could understand it, and were more open to the influence of justice than of grace. When, by the discipline of history and the teaching of prophets, they were better able to understand higher conceptions, higher came, but only by Him who realized perfect manhood was the perfect Godhead made known. And the higher the notion of God rose, the higher grew the notion of man. Man must rightly conceive himself to respect himself, and his progress may best be measured by his suc-

cessive ideas of his own nature. He is to himself, the older he gets, only the more mysterious; his being is a miniature universe, surrounded with all the mysteries of the vaster. We cannot forget that we once were not, that we soon shall not be; great eternity lies behind, an eternity no less great lies before; boundless immensity surrounds us; and we, small, self-conscious, rise like marvellous islets of life out of the immeasurable reaches of eternity, and feel washed by the wide spaces of immensity. Every man who has ever speculated much, has stood silent, fearful, before that thought of himself, feeling as if his little self-conscious being trembled like a solitary point of light in depths of unfathomable darkness. All the great thinkers of antiquity, indeed, of all time, have felt the mystery of personal being, and have thought of it as holding within it the secret of the universe. A great teacher, one who lately passed away from us, in one of the many wonderful paragraphs of his most characteristic work, has described this humanity of ours as "Emerging, like a God-created, fire-breathing spirit-host, from the Inane; as hastening stormfully across the astonished earth, and plunging again into the Inane. Earth's mountains are levelled and her seas filled up, in our passage; can the earth, which is but dead and a vision, resist spirits which have reality and are alive? On the hardest adamant some footprint of us is stamped in; the last rear of the host will read traces of the earliest van. But whence? O, heaven, whither? Sense knows not; faith knows not; only that it is through mystery to mystery, from God and to God."

> "We are such stuff
> As dreams are made on, and our little life
> Is rounded with a sleep!"

Now, think of the soft transforming light the Christian faith has by its conception of God shed upon the idea of man, and the stern mystery of human life, its source and destiny. Man is son of the Eternal Father, and everlasting son; he is spirit, for God is spirit. The thought he incarnates is ever seeking the thought incarnated in all material being, and working in all historical movements. Man who is thought, finding thought all around him, feels in the midst of these great infinities at home. But the homeliness becomes sweeter and diviner when he knows himself a filial spirit, with God as the paternal. His eternity becomes our eternity; to sense this universe is a dark and insoluble mystery, but to spirit that knows God it is light, for He is Light. No moment in eternity, no point in space can be terrible to the soul that loves to be at home with the Eternal, and knows that His home is everywhere and every moment. Where the conscious Son is, there is the besetting Father. We issued forth from no Inane, but from the bosom of Infinite Love; we vanish into no Inane, but are received into those divine hands that love to hold and welcome the spirit that trusts. "Thou hast made us for Thyself," said Augustine, "and our hearts are restless till they repose in Thee." The heart at peace with God can taste no trouble, for it finds all things in all places work together for its good.

3. But now, how are God and man related? The simplest duty of the son is love; nothing is more beautiful or simple than filial piety. The joy of the father is affection, his delight is to secure the happiness of his child. In the religions of man we see man's tendency to God, his search after Him. The search, indeed, is often painful, the track is marked with blood. In one aspect the study of religions is a most humiliating study, because it shows what dark, what dismal ideas of Deity, and painful methods of reaching and pleasing Him have prevailed among men. I often sympathise with the Roman Lucretius, when, looking at religion as it was in his day, he spoke of it as lowering upon mortals with a hideous aspect, as pressing human life down under its inexorable foot. For if you look at the way in which man has conceived God and tried to please Him, you will find it hard at times to admire his religion. Take one rite— human sacrifice. Think what horror and pain must have been associated with Deity in the minds of those who could give the fruit of their body for the sin of the soul! There is a wondrous Greek tragedy that tells how the great hero, Agamemnon, offered up his daughter Iphigenia, that he might win from the gods a favourable breeze to waft the Greek ships to the Trojan shore. It was little wonder that the Greek poets saw in that sacrifice an act that, while it might

please Deity, yet offended the moral order of the universe, and awoke the Eumenides, the dread unslumbering furies, who bring retribution to man. Where men seek to please God by outraging heart and conscience, religion has become perverted from a universal good to the basest evil ; and, as I said before, human sacrifices were known to almost all the old religions, as indeed they are known to many heathen worships to-day. Remember the fundamental principle, as is the god so is the religion, and you will see that human sacrifice but expresses or represents the idea of God in these heathen faiths.

Yet it, no less, represents another idea, man's sense of sin, of ill-desert, of inability by character or conduct to please God. There is no sterner fact in human experience than the guilty conscience ; the man who is not saved from it becomes its victim, it depraves him and darkens all his world. If his religion does not deliver him from it, it debases the religion. Yet does not this only the more help us to see the miserable ideas of Deity that prevailed among the most cultured peoples ? They did not think so well of God that they could conceive of God saving them, pitying and helping them the more for their awful consciousness of misery and sin. Instead they had to win his favour, win it by pain, by suffering, by surrendering to what they most feared the object they most loved. If we think of these things need we wonder that heathen men should have despised their gods and hated religion ?

4. But now see how strangely and beautifully changed and dissimilar the Christian notion is. Here God does not demand the sacrifice, He makes it; He does not extort blood, does not delight in suffering and death; He gives, and the giving is a passion to Him. He so loves the world that He gives for its life His only-begotten Son. The great sacrifice is one not demanded from man, it is given of God; His is the act and His, too, the design to bring man home, to win the prodigal, who is still a son, from his misery, and shame, and sin, to the light and life and love of the Father's house. Under Moses God gave the law, and the law came with its severity, the dread threatening that every sin had its appropriate penalty. But under Christ God gives His love, that He may the more completely win man's. The idea was a development when viewed in relation to the Old Testament religion; but it is a contrast, nay a contradiction, to all the other religions man has ever professed. It is, indeed, a contradiction that but brings out at once the grandeur and the uniqueness of the Christian conception. It shows the moral energy of God exercised, not in the way of retribution, but in the way of redemption; it shows the sovereign working in the way of the Father, stooping unto utmost sacrifice that He might save and restore man.

And the form in which He works this glorious redemption is remarkable. It is in His Son, in and through One who bears the nature of man, and is in that nature the image of the invisible God. Deity does not dwell remote, aloof, apart from man, He is around, He is about, He is within, He has lifted human nature into connexion and kinship with the Divine. The Son who suffers for us dignifies the nature in which he suffers. In condemning sin He exalts humanity; ever since man through Christ learned the great secret — the kinship of his humanity with Deity, see how that humanity has risen out of the dust, become conscious of the Divine affinities within it, and striven towards the realization of its more glorious possibilities.

Thus in the doctrine of the incarnation the great truth is implied, that man is bound by kinship, by fellowship of nature to the God who is his Father. What shows us the descent of God to man, shows us also the ascent of man to God; He who came down into our humanity, lowly as His outward form seemed, has more than all the sages of the world given us an idea of our humanity that ennobles each individual man.

IV

We must now turn from these beliefs in themselves, and look at their action in and through the Christian religion as it appears in history. We have seen Christ's idea of religion in His own person, and in His teaching. We have also seen the great cardinal beliefs on which it reposed. We have now to see how these were or ought to be expressed, articulated, and embodied in the Christian religion.

1. And we had better begin this new discussion by looking first at their action on the ideal of humanity. Now note, Christ created the idea of humanity; it was not till He made it; it was His creation, He spoke, and it stood up a living thing. Two great classes of forces, which we may call centrifugal, had hitherto prevented, as in many places they still prevent, the ideal of humanity from being realized and understood. The first of these orders of forces was the national. Men are divided into nations, and nations are divided by race, by language and by religion. The differences of nation and race, and language, can be overcome, but differences of religion are radical; where they stand, men can never meet as brothers. If men differ in colour, in blood, and in speech, they may still recognize common manhood, but as a matter of history, common manhood has never been recognized save through common religion, and the only common religion which has made men recognize their common humanity has been that of Christ.

The second great class of centrifugal forces are social, they are caste, rank, blood, class, money, culture —all the thousand things that make men of the same race, language, and religion feel as if they were yet divided into a multitude of separate cliques or sects. These divisions find in certain religions their highest sanction. The Brahmanism of to-day has no unity of worship or of faith, its distinctive characteristic is its system of castes, the deep and impassable lines by which it distinguishes men who speak the same language, and live under the same laws.

Now the Christian is the only religion that in history and in idea has opposed and victoriously contended against these social, separative, and disintegrative forces. For Islam is in this respect secondary and derivative; its universalism but illustrates and confirms the Christian. The idea of Roman citizenship when extended to the provincials seemed to create equality, but the fact of Roman slavery cancelled and repealed it. The idea of humanity could not be created by external machinery, like the action of an imperial policy; it could only grow out of a conception of man's nature, and the relations in which he stood as a whole to the Creator. The peculiarity of Christ's action was that it modified man from within; it made humanity one by its doctrine of God on the one hand, and of human sonship on the other. What was the very first thing that the greatest of the Christian apostles said to the most cultivated of the heathens? "God hath made of one blood all nations of men, for to dwell on all the face of the earth." When he addressed the Christian communities, what did he say? "In Christ there is neither Greek nor Jew, circumcision nor uncircumcision, Barbarian, Scythian, bond nor free, but Christ is all and in all." And what did this mean? The distinctions of race had perished before the universal religion; at its bidding humanity stood forth as one, a brotherhood. So the unity of man meant fraternity; men who were sons of God, who called God Father, were brothers. Brotherhood necessarily involved equality; where fraternity reigned, slavery could have no place, the sons of the free home must themselves be free. With freedom there came the right of man to seek God, to speak to Him, to live according to the will He revealed in His word and to the conscience; and therefore the right men call of private judgment, the right to think and speak the thoughts man holds most true. But where men were conceived to be one, a brotherhood, equal and free, there the duty emerged of common love and common service The men God loved, man was bound to love, where He willed good, man was bound to do it; without love of man no love of God was possible, without service of man there could be no service which God approved.

Out of this ideal grew the great notion of a divine society, humanity organized into a city or state that should perfectly express and realize the will of God. The Christian ideal or thought of the city of God had no parallel in any religion or system of antiquity. Had I time I would sketch for you the greatest ideal of a perfect society known to the ancient world,—perhaps, outside Christ, the greatest ideal known to the modern,—the dream Plato incarnated in his "Republic." Were it possible I could have wished to unsphere the spirit of Plato, and call him from those worlds that hold

> "The immortal mind that hath forsook
> Her mansion in this fleshly nook,"

that he might teach us how he, the greatest of the Greeks, conceived and would realize the ideal state. Think where he lived, in the fairest land of antiquity, under the brightest sun, amid the most cultivated people, pupil of the greatest teacher and philosopher of his race, associated with the wisest statesmen, heir to an heroic past, moved by a poetry that is still the joy of the scholar, and then conceive him turning in his maturest manhood to think out the model of a perfect republic. And what was it? It was a state where there was to be little freedom, for philosophers were to be kings—and a strange king the philosopher always makes, for he is a man resolute to fit men into his theory, and his best theory is, you may be well assured, a bad frame for the simplest man. And the state these philosophers were to rule was to be one where the home was destroyed, where women were to be held in common, where there was to be a community of goods, where life was to be regulated by rules and hard fixed methods that would have allowed no elasticity, no play for glad and spontaneous energy. That Republic could not have been realized without the ruin of humanity, and was possible at its best only for the Greek, was conceived in derision of the barbarian, and afforded even to Greek nature only the poorest exercise.

Turn now to the ideal Christ created. It lifted all men, through its doctrine of God and the Redeemer, into a unity that was a brotherhood, and involved an equality of rights on the one hand and a sovereignty of duty on the other. It left the mother and the wife and the daughter to make glad and enlarge the spirit of the husband and the father, to evoke and ennoble the soul of the son. It left the man to be while the citizen, the husband, while the husband, the brother of his kind, the servant in his age of the everlasting God. It left the state where it stood, but it changed all the citizens, ennobled them, made them simpler, truer men; and through this change of the men altogether changed the state. It aimed at the good of all, through seeking the good of each, by blessing the one it laboured to bless the many. Whatever meant misery to man the Christian was to relieve, whatever meant wrong he was to redress. They say that Christ has nothing to do with questions of state; what concerns the conduct of nations or of peoples does not concern Him. No saying less true could any man utter; all questions of state, all social and civil politics are to me questions of religion. And such they must be to the man who wishes to realize on earth the kingdom of God. Never, while an abuse tarries, while a hate reigns, while a barbarism remains unconquered, never, while ignorance broods with its dark and jealous wing over the mind of man, while injustice or unequal law or disorder or wrong live on earth can the Christian man be still or inactive in the arena of public life. All without as within us must be brought into harmony with the great law of Christ, and only as the harmony of the renewed spirit is reflected in the renewed humanity will the glorious dream of the city of God be realized.

2. This brings us, secondly, to Christ's method of realizing the ideal of humanity. His method, indeed, is very simple, but it is remarkable in its strength. That method does not proceed by ignoring the hardest and most painful facts of our human experience. Christ was open-eyed as regards the actual state of our nature and world. He knew it was miserable, altogether evil, but He did not mean to skin the sore. He said, as He laid His finger on the evil, " This sore must be healed, sin is, and sin must be vanquished." No religion has so great a sense of sin and at the same time of salvation. The sense of sin indeed is almost shared in its intensity by another than the religion of Christ, that of Buddha. Buddha was a beautiful spirit, a character of rare pity and gentleness, touched to his inmost soul by sorrow for sin, and at the sight of human misery. And his whole system was inspired with the desire to deliver man from the sorrow he hated—but how deliver him? By freeing him from being, by bringing him to a death that was annihilation. He saved men by destroying man, and he magnified sin that he might only the more pour contempt on life. But what of Christ? His sense of sin had for background His exalted ideal of man; it was because man was so

noble that his sin was so terrible. And what did He aim at? Vanquishing the sin, but saving the man. If you throw away a life that you may deliver from disease, what does it mean but that you do not care for the person whose life it is. But if you die to conquer the disease and save the person, does it not mean that your hatred of disease is only the reverse side of your love of life? Christ's aversion to sin but expresses His love of man, and the glorious peculiarity of His method was this—while He vanquished the sin He saved the man.

It is well to look at Christ's peculiarity in this matter. Men in face of sin may be divided into various classes. There is the Cynic; he is a common person in these days; our clubs make him; they are great factors of cynicism. Where amid much comfort you can talk scandal, indulge wit, and derive comfort from the scorn in which you hold weaker men—it is easy and natural to be a cynic. The cynic has ever risen in days like these, he was in Christ's time and before it, as he is now, and said then as he says now, "What a poor thing is man! A compound of meanness and vanity, and whether his meanness or his vanity be most to be despised, it is hard to tell, yet were it not for this compound, what should we have to laugh at, what to make life pleasant?" The cynic little dreams that in so despising man, he but shows himself despicable. Yet it is ever so; the faultiest men quickly see and severely condemn their own faults when reflected in another's face.

Then there is the Epicurean, the man who loves pleasure, who hates alike the thought and the experience of pain. To be burdened with a sense of man's misery, is but to have his own pleasure marred, and so he says : " Why trouble ourselves about a state we cannot mend ; man will be foolish ; let him be a fool, while we here can at least make our own lives pleasant, and so lessen the pain of humanity by securing and enlarging our own happiness."

Then there is the Stoic, who believes in the sanity of Nature and the sufficiency of man to obey the laws contained within it. And so he speaks thus : " Virtue is beautiful, the man who is not virtuous is a creature to be pitied ; he belongs to the lowest type of men, for he contradicts and defeats the nature by virtue of which he is Man. But our virtue is our own, evolved by our own action from within ourselves ; let us cultivate virtue, and so, by showing its beauty, make it attractive, only let our calm never be broken by the restless passion that would suffer for the evil. The weaker must always be, but to the stronger they ought only to be conditions for the exercise of his calmer strength."

These are the criticisms of selfishness, the doctrines of impotence. Virtue that will not suffer to save man, is but decent vice. There is no parsimony so miserable as the one whose chief concern is personal happiness. But even men of these types have often, especially under the influence of Christian ideals, become zealous doers of good, helpers of humanity, and let us give all honour to men ruled, even though they may not know it, by the Spirit of Christ, who follow Him in any degree even while they do not honour His name.

But observe Christ's peculiarity ; He stood alone, and His religion stands alone here—He was a Redeemer, His religion is a religion of redemption. It sees sin, and it hates sin, but to it every sinner is a man that may be saved. To save him Christ lived and died, to save him the Spirit of God works and wills, to save him every good man ought to labour and to watch. The passion of Christ is the symbol of His religion, it suffers everywhere for the sin of humanity, but in order to the deliverance of the humanity that has sinned. The state of estrangement from God, God wills to change into a state of reconciliation, and the religion of Christ is the means that works it ; and it is of all the religions the only one that is in the true and proper sense a religion of redemption.

V

Now, the thing that chiefly concerns us about this religion of redemption, is the way in which it affects the personal and collective life of man.

1. Well, then, mark how it restores the depraved nature into the image of its Creator, and makes it as redeemed a vehicle of the Divine purposes, a factor of the order and ends of God. Now I would just note three simple historical facts in relation to Christ's

redemptive action. He has proved Himself in His handling of men possessed of three great powers. First : an unparalleled power to change men, to make bad men good. Secondly : an unparalleled power to make the men He has reformed into factors of good —agents of redemption. Thirdly : an unparalleled power to associate the men He has redeemed into societies with larger ideas than the states of earth, societies with an ideal and mission of their own, or rather, one that is altogether His. In proof of His possession of these gifts I would appeal to history. I ask you this : Where will you find three men who have more profoundly affected the history of the world than Peter, Paul and John ? What were they ? Peter, when Jesus found him, was an ignorant, impulsive, superstitious fisherman, plying his craft on the sea of Galilee, without thought or vision of the greater world around. John was a brother fisherman, rather more cultivated and refined perhaps, yet with hardly more promise of capability and power. Paul, when Jesus found him, was a tentmaker, poor, mean in bodily appearance, possibly painful to look at, certainly no person a passer-by would have selected as a manifest king of men. But just see what these three men, coming under the influence of Christ, became and did. Peter conducts himself before priests and rulers like a statesman, founds and administers churches with the wisdom of a far-seeing ruler of men. John writes the most marvellous history on record, serenest, clearest, profoundest, fullest of insight into the secret springs of life and action in God, tenderest in the delicate portraiture of the Christ he knew, most awful and graphic in its description of the men that plotted his death, and accomplished it. Paul becomes the author of Epistles that command the mind, that have made and governed the thought of the cultivated peoples of these Christian centuries. And these three are but typical. In every age this marvellous power that Christ possesses has stood expressed and declared in great persons. The creative personalities of the Christian centuries are of Christ's making, and as He made the persons, so He has ruled their conduct and their lives. The order of history since He lived has been an order He has guided, especially in all that has made for human grace and good. He who has been so able to change men and make them factors of good for man has indeed been proved by transcendent fact our great Redeemer.

2. What I think of the action of Christian men and societies in history will in later lectures become apparent. But let the creative personalities of the Christian centuries, the men with a passion for the good of man, witness to the distinctive power of Christ. In Himself we see what He means man to be to man; in the men He has formed, who have lived under the inspiration of His love, we see the sort of service He has rendered to humanity in history, one of the ways in which he has ameliorated our common lot. Deeds are greater than words.

Men may find parallels to sayings of the New Testament in Confucius or in Buddha, in Plato or in Seneca, but one thing they cannot parallel, the achievements of Christ in the region of human personalities. Here He has been the Supreme Creator, one who dwells altogether alone. Do not think that Buddha can stand by His side. The person so named was, as I have said, a gentle and beautiful human character, oppressed by the sense of human suffering, laden with sorrow at the thought of the miserable and illusive life to which man was doomed; but he had not the love of life that turned all man's moral energies into forces that worked for its amelioration. Buddha so hated life as to extinguish the very desire to mend it; Christ so loved life as to create in all who loved Him the desire for its ennoblement. The men who have most imitated Buddha have preached a gospel of annihilation; the men who have best known Christ have preached a gospel of salvation, of grace that reigns through righteousness unto eternal life. The aim of Buddha was to make men know their misery that they might be willing to lay down the burden of existence, but the purpose of Christ was to make men conscious of sin that they might live unto holiness, forsake the darkness and seek the light. To Buddha the highest life was the secluded, the renunciation of the familiar duties of society and the home; but to Christ the holiest life was the life of active beneficence, the piety that helped our neighbour, that honoured God by serving man. The secret of His power was His love of man; the men that love Him must love as He loved, and so translate into the realities of personal character and social conduct the health, the holiness, the wholeness of His glorious ideal.

3. I know there are men in England who use base words when they speak of our Christianity. It is to you, working men, that they make their appeal. Now, in matters of this kind, we can only concern ourselves with men who use honourable and veracious speech; with those whose language is but buffoonery, and the brutal buffoonery of poltroons, we can have no concern whatever. The great heart of the world is just, and, turning from the ignorant and rancorous men, who fight with the poisoned weapons of savages or slaves, I cry across the ages to the mighty spirits of the Christian centuries, "What think ye of Christ?" The poets, led by the great Florentine, the man of sad, lone spirit, of face so beautiful, yet so full of wondrous thought, who imagined the strange circles of the *Inferno*, and yet saw as in open vision the celestial "Mount of light," while Chaucer, in his quaint English guise, and Shakespeare, "Fancy's sweetest child," and Milton, whose voice had a sound as of the sea, and Cowper, and Coleridge, and Wordsworth, and many another bright spirit follow in his train—make answer, "He was the soul of our poetry, our inspiration, and our joy." "What think ye of Christ?" we ask the men of thought, and out of the middle ages rise the schoolmen whose mighty

intellects made light in its darkness, the founders of Modern Philosophy, Descartes, and Bacon, and Locke, the foremost minds of the eighteenth century, the century of unbelief, Leibnitz, and Newton, and Berkeley, and Kant; the thinkers, too, that in sheer intellectual force transcend all the other men of this century of conscious wisdom, Schelling and Hegel, and they altogether confess and acknowledge " the Christ stands alone, pre-eminent, only Son of God among men." "What think ye of Christ?" we ask the great philanthropists, the men who have made our laws kindlier while more just to the criminal, our prisons more wholesome while more deterrent of crime, who have accomplished the liberation of the slave, who have made us conscious of our duties to savage peoples abroad and to our lapsed at home; the men who in these centuries have been foremost in doing good and in guiding to nobleness the mind of man, and Bernard and Francis of Assisi, John Howard and Mrs. Fry, Wilberforce and Livingstone, surrounded by the noble band of all our good Samaritans, answer with one accord, " Without Him we should have been without our inspiration and our strength, the love of man and the hatred of wrong that have constrained us to our work." "What think ye of Christ?" we cry to the great masters of music and song, who have woven for us the divine speech of the Oratorio, and filled the air with harmonies grander than any nature has known, and they for answer but bid us read the names of their supreme works,

"Messiah," "St. Paul," "Redemption," and know that but for Christ the one art in which the modern has far transcended the ancient world would never have been. "What think ye of Christ?" we ask the painters who have made the canvas live with their ideals of love and holiness, pity and suffering; the sculptors who have chiselled the shapeless marble into forms so noble as to need only speech to be the living man made perfect; and their great leaders, from famed Giotto through Fra Angelico to Michael Angelo and Raphael, down to our own Reynolds and Ruskin, send forth the response, "He has been the soul of our art, our dream by night, our joy by day, to paint Him worthily were the highest, though, alas, most hopeless feat of man." O, yes; thou Christ the Redeemer, Son of God yet Son of Man, stand forth in Thy serene and glorious power, Leader of our progress, Author of all our good, ideal and inspiration of all our right and righteousness, and reign over the hearts and in the lives of men!

IV

THE CHRISTIAN RELIGION IN THE FIRST FIFTEEN CENTURIES OF ITS EXISTENCE

WHAT we have to attempt this evening is to study the action of the religion of Christ in the first fifteen centuries of its existence. That is an immense subject, quite sufficient in itself to awe and oppress any one's spirit. To make the attempt to discuss or describe it in an hour's discourse, is certainly to exhibit a courage more allied to adventure than to discretion. What, too, is intended, is the more difficult, as we must attempt to get below the surface at the underlying principles or causes, that we may the better discover their nature, their action, and their end.

It were easy to write or to tell the history of a Church, but it is not so easy to describe the history of a Religion. Yet, to the partial, or partisan, or careless historian, or to the designing polemic, these are identical, to be treated as one and the same. Here they are to be held as throughout distinct; as though often blended in action, yet as different as are form and matter. It is needful that we see that what runs back into Christ, or follows by necessary consequence from Him, and from the circle of truths He created, and whose centre He is, is of the essence of the Christian Religion ; but what springs from the needs, the ambitions, the interests of any Christian Society, is the Society's alone.

I do not stand here as the apologist of any church, least of all of those churches that to me, in many points, fundamentally misconceive and misinterpret the very idea, as in many respects they have perverted and depraved the reality, of the religion of Christ. What I wish to do is simply this, to see how that religion has acted in history, how it has affected the happiness, the progress, the wellbeing of society and of man. In the nineteen centuries of its existence, it has furnished, on the most stupendous scale, experimental proof of its intrinsic character, contents, and qualities. In spite of manifold and most burdensome impedimenta, it has changed everything, man most of all ; and every change it has, as a religion, worked, has worked altogether for good. We know what the world was when Christianity entered it, we know what it is to-day, and at every moment between then and now, we can trace the history and action of the great Christian ideas or truths, now acting in secret, now openly, now receiving the merciless hate of a mighty empire, now collecting, directing, penetrating, as with the passion of God, the concentrated enthusiasms of peoples. And if we are to understand matters aright, we must compare what was with what is, and find in what way Christianity has worked to change what was into what is; and only when that has been done, can we be in a position to answer the question—has it acted in the common life of man as a divine religion ought to act? have its fruits been but the apples of Sodom, or have they been indeed living grapes from the living vine planted in the paradise of God?

I hope it is not necessary to restate the purpose of these lectures. They were intended, not to deal with doubt on the one hand, or doctrine on the other, but simply to exhibit the action of religion in history, with a view to discover its true relation to the great economical, industrial, and political problems that interest the working men of to-day. This is a work which I think you have a right to ask from the men who study and teach the religion of Jesus Christ. Here are Christian men and churches faced with Nihilism, Socialism, Secularism, and many another form of negation, or passionate unbelief, often more remarkable for the intensity of its bigotry and the density of its ignorance than any other quality besides. I have meanwhile no wish to deal with these as a critic on the one hand, or an apologist on the other. It were an easy thing to grapple with their assumptions and their ignorance, and handle them after the manner of the apologetical protagonist. But my purpose is quite other. If they are, *why* are they? There is a reason for their being. Have they not in this and other lands been born of disappointed hopes? Men have a right to expect that religion, as Christian religion, shall cure poverty, shall make the charity that is at once the luxury of the rich and the misery of the poor, cease ; shall bring a time when wealth, equally distributed, shall create the happiest of civil and social and secular states. And much of our Nihilism and our Socialism has been born of disappointed hopes, and hopes that were legitimate. And the Christian churches, if they are wise, will not simply play the part of apologist, and say to these people, "How false and futile are your beliefs, ill-considered, inconsequent, incoherent, formed without knowledge, maintained without science, a bundle of mere illiterate dogmatisms ; " but, though, unhappily, all this may be true, they will say, "We are to blame for these crude negations ; they are the children of our neglect, the Nemesis that has followed on the heels of our unfulfilled duties. They do not represent the rebellion of reason, but it is a rebellion with a reason, for it has not been caused by dislike to the truth of God, but by the inaction or impotence of His churches." Then, turning to the great and fruitful idea of religion, the vital truths and realities of faith, they will ask, "What do they mean for life ? what message have they to the multitudes of men who toil and spin, and how are we to build up in the world, and in view of man and mankind, a state, a society that, in all its parts, shall express and declare the great ideal of a city of God, a society in harmony with His spirit and mind ? "

Now, my attempt hitherto has been to bring out the principles and qualities in religion as an idea, and in the religions of the Old and the New Testaments, creative of a happier order, contributory to a wealthier state, and a more progressive society; and I wish to-night, to try to discover how the Christian religion, even in its earliest birth, has affected these same great forces, and worked towards these great purposes and ends.

Let me begin then, by simply stating that it is here necessary to look at the Christian religion from three points of view. 1. As regards some of the distinctive notes or qualities it possessed at its birth, or on its appearance in the world. 2. At the way in which the Christian societies were affected by certain old Pagan and Judaic ideas; and 3. At the way in which, in spite of these, the Christian truths or ideas so worked through the Christian Societies as to affect for good the common life of man, our industrial and economical systems, and our toiling men and multitudes.

I

Now, you will note, beginning with the first, that Christianity at its birth stood a centre of new ideas, a circle of great and splendid beliefs. Some of these, cardinal and central for our question, were exhibited in the previous lecture. Those meant specially concerned the new ideas of God, of man, and of the method of reconciling God and man. These were such as to make man the glorious vehicle or organ for fulfilling or carrying out to completion the divine purpose or plan in history. Growing directly out of those ideas, or truths, or beliefs, came these qualities :—

1. Christianity was a universal, not a national religion. As universal, it was something generically new, absolutely unlike all that had been before, or were around. A universal religion is a religion capable of living anywhere and everywhere, suited to men of all classes and in all stages of their development, capable of satisfying the largest, yet of stooping to the meanest nature ; yet able so to fill the nature as to make it dissatisfied with its attainment, ever craving after something nobler and higher. A universal is more than a missionary religion. It must be missionary, but all missionary are not universal religions. Buddhism is missionary, yet we can see this, that it so hates life, it so hates society, it so dislikes whatever tends to create an order that shall prolong and lift the life of humanity, as to act as a sort of paralysis of progress, as to produce a sort of general collapse in all the more progressive and ameliorative agencies of time. Islam is missionary, but then it spreads not simply by power, but so as to deprave the civilized, as to lower the higher and nobler races. A universal religion must be one that can help man ever forward, enlarge his nature, give him for ever the idea that far as he has come he has yet an infinite path to travel to a higher and nobler perfection.

Now the universalism of Christianity rose out of its cardinal ideas. The one God made mankind one. One God and one humanity could be expressed only by one religion. Now, mark, that was at first an unintelligible idea. To the early world all religions were local. Zeus could not be understood out of Greece, Jupiter could not be understood out of Rome. The Roman might carry his faith with him, but it was bound up with the being of his state, with the idea of his city. No man can be a Brahman out of India. If he comes here he loses so much of his Brahmanism that he has to be purged and purified at his return. There was not then, as there is not now, any religion, but the religion of Christ that possessed universalism, that could be anywhere by any man believed and obeyed, and that tended to embrace all men in a glorious unity. That made it a most insoluble problem, a strange anomaly, to men possessed of the older ideas, and many a great historian and thinker stood puzzled and helpless before the notion that a faith could be universal, that there could be a religion expressing faith in one God, one Humanity, and one great Mediator between them.

2. The second distinctive note was spiritual. It was purely spiritual, alike as regards its matter and its independence of all outer and local forms. Every old religion, as has been explained, had its temples, its priests, its hierarchy, its augurs, its processions, its sacrifices, the varied signs and symbols by which

externally it lived. But now here was the wonderful anomaly. Christ was no priest, appointed no man a priest, erected no temple, established no ritual, laid down no law of sacrifice, enjoined no sacrifice but the sacrifice of clean hands and a pure heart, a holy and noble life unto God. Now its independence of all sacerdotal forms made His religion a greater anomaly than its Founder, more wonderful, less intelligible. That it should be without a priest, without a priesthood, without an altar, without a temple for a home, made it seem to the ancient Greeks, Romans, and Jews, a religion?—nay, an atheism, an utter denial of all religious belief. And so, why were the Christians condemned to the lions? Why were they forced to the amphitheatre? They were said to be Atheists, men profane, without God, while in truth, they were so spiritually religious that the unspiritual religions could not understand them. And bigoted, intolerant, as all heathen religions were, the Roman doomed the Christians, as men godless and atheistic, to the stake.

But not only so; the religion was independent of all political organizations, all hierarchical and graduated orders. By that I mean this—the polities now thought so cardinal to the religion had no existence in its purest and most historical form, the primitive state of the religion as it issued from the mind of its Founder and the hands of His apostles. Men say, Christianity is papacy. Nay, papacy was fatal to many things in the cardinal Christian idea.

The father is an excellent authority when his family are children ; but once the family is grown they must not be treated as infants. Papacy making men spiritual infants stands in the way of the realization of the highest Christian idea, which is essentially the religion of manhood, and speaks to men as men. And as with papacy, so with all hierarchical forms. They were later, they did not belong to the early Church. The earliest was a society where men taught, men learned and lived, each after his own kind. The man who believed became a member of Christ. Becoming a member of Christ, he became a worker for man ; and those little communities that rose in those ancient cities that stood round the tideless Mediterranean, what were they, every one of them, but missionary societies formed of men who lived in the most devoted way for man, to cure his sorrow, to heal his misery, to help his sin, to bring all into holier relations to God ? The abolition of the old sacerdotalism was the creation of a grand spiritual religion formed from heaven.

3. That brings us to the third great quality. The religion was a religion creative and regulative of a new life, both individual and collective. Now, as has been stated over and over again, the ancient religions did not pretend to give a moral law, directive of personal and social and civil life. The moralist was never the priest, he was always the philosopher. No man did good because his religion bound him. No, it was only the maxims of the schools that could

direct and teach. If you want to find the highest ideal of morality in Pagan times, where do you go? Certainly not to the oracles, certainly not to the mysteries, certainly not to the priesthoods. Nay, but you go to the academy, to the porch, or to the grove, and say to Plato, or Zeno, or Aristotle, "Teach me how to regulate my life." And as there was no morality connected with the religion, so the gods did not concern themselves about morality. A Pagan moralist could say, "The gods give me life and fortune, but a cheerful, contented spirit I secure for myself." Or he could say, "The gods send war and pestilence, and we offer sacrifices to propitiate their wrath; but the virtuous man is sufficient for himself, he needs no help of the gods."

Now the result was inevitable; where religion had no concern with morality, morality could draw from it no inspiration. But when Christ appeared, these were bound together in indissoluble marriage, the highest moral principle and the highest religious faith were united in eternal alliance. And the result was seen at once; first in this: man was placed in the centre of new moral forces, new moral forces were placed within the man. Then happened a wonderful thing. Where the schools had been powerless, Christianity became powerful, and men who never felt the inspiration to a good and noble life felt it now.

And, as a second result, the virtues were universalized. If you had wished to scandalize an ancient philosopher, you could not have done it more effectually than by associating him with the unlettered, with the people. Celsus, the great assailant of the Christian faith, held up the Christians to scorn because they were unlettered men, slaves, cobblers, weavers, men who were not equal to stand in an Academy, or speak in elegant Greek. But therein lay its power, it took the poor, the outcast, the despised, and it made them more moral than the schools had made the philosophers. You will get many a beautiful proverb in Seneca, you will get many a fine ethical principle in Plato, you will find in Stoicism some of the most exalted precepts that human ethics have ever known. But mark you one thing, you will never discover that these elevated the common life of man, affected the course of lust, made the bad good, or the impure holy. Where they failed, Christ succeeded with splendid, glorious success; He made out of the very outcasts men that became saints to God.

And then followed a third thing. Virtues new and beautiful were created. Now I don't mean to compare the Greek "Eros," the Latin "Amor," and the Christian "Love." The man who knows classic life knows that the distance between these is an infinite distance. Love, what did it signify to the ancient world but a form of lust, or what at best carried with it every connotation of passion and its pain? But Love, what does it become to Christian man? Read that wonderful chapter which stands as the xiii. of first Corinthians, the glorious description of Christian love, the power that can inspire, can regulate, can ennoble man, making him live for his fellows the wide world over. Or take another thing, take the tenderness it brought into life, of man to woman, of strong to weak. There is no grander ancient character than Socrates, beautiful character he is in many a way. He, citizen, thinker, teacher, plying that wondrous dialectic craft of his in the streets of Athens, is a form attractive to all eyes. And he is so attractive because he stands out from among the crowd the creator of a new moral ideal, at once stronger, higher, and more humane than the old epic and heroic ideal embodied in the Homeric Achilles. But now, look how over against him stands the image of Xanthippe, his wife. She has had hard measure dealt to her; his contemporaries and historians have made her seem one who led the poor philosopher a hardish life, and have made her the type of a woman who makes life not pleasant to the man that has wedded her. And many a dry-as-dust commentator has grown somewhat humorous over the sweet relief that death brought to Socrates when it saved him from Xanthippe.

But if you examine the simple truth as it stands in history, that woman has no right to be so rated; the man, on the other hand, reason to be rated most soundly. His love is all for the state and not for the home, marriage is for him only a convenient institution, carrying with it no duties of living affection, of mutual helpfulness and cheerful intercourse, and his conduct was but too good an exponent of his opinions. He cultivated an admiring friendship for Aspasia, but he had only the coldest neglect for poor Xanthippe. His duties are all to Athens and Greece, and not at all to home. He puns, questions, teaches for the good of philosophy and the state, but she has to provide for their children. She goes to him in the hour of death, grieved, distressed in a woman's way, and he sits as in the Phædo, sublimely discoursing with his friends. When she comes he never feels a bit the loss to her, they do not feel the pain to the woman and to the children; nay, it is going to trouble the serenity of the philosopher to see the woman who was his wife, and the children she had borne him. And they send her away with no word of comfort, with scorn rather than with cheer. There now stands out clear and distinct one of the great differences the religion of Christ brought in, it brought in the spirit of love, made the weak dependent on the strong, made the strong thoughtful of the weak, made the man in his might, in his manhood, with all the rights of manhood upon him, be to the weak generous, and to the dependent noble. This is but one phase of its action in universalizing and creating a higher virtue, and so purifying and perfecting the whole notion of society. The state of life built up in harmony with these principles, according to these great ideals could not but be a kindlier, nobler, humaner state.

4. Imagine, then, Christianity launched on the stream. It has those features we have sketched,

and how has it to live and do its work? By means of the preacher, the teacher, the man that persuades the reason. That, too, made it something new. A man like Gibbon has represented the old religions as tolerant. I stand here to say that no ancient religion was tolerant, or could be tolerant. It was in the heart of it a narrow nationalism, and it could allow to live within the nation only the men that supported it. Why was Socrates done to death? Religion, as the ancients understood it, persecuted him thereto. Or why was Protagoras banished from Athens, in spite of the friendship and protection of Pericles, the most illustrious statesman of Athens in her most illustrious age? Because he had ventured, in a treatise on the gods, to say, " I do not know whether the gods do or do not exist." To express such a doubt was to become liable to the last penalty; and Protagoras preferred exile to death. But, perhaps, you may think Rome better than Greece. Well, take Maecenas, the man Horace so greatly praises, and get at his advice to Augustus. What does he say? He tells Augustus that whatever he tolerates he is not to tolerate alien religions, he is not to allow his people to break from the ancient faith. But it may be thought, this man was no true Roman and lover of liberty, rather he was the friend and admirer of the new emperor, advising him how best to found a despotism on the ruins of the ancient freedom. Let us appeal, then, to Cicero, and we find him in his treatise on Laws saying, that no man shall be allowed to worship any gods except those publicly recognized by law; or let us ask the distinguished Roman jurist, Julius Paulus, what he understands to be the law on this matter? and he explicitly enough answers, "Whoever introduces new and unknown religions, by which the minds of men may be disturbed, are, if belonging to the higher ranks, to be banished, but if to the lower, they are to receive the penalty of death." These principles of Roman law made the persecution of the Christians not only legal, but necessary; and they stood associated with the fundamental idea and condition of the Roman state. To doubt the state religion, was to doubt the right of the state to be, its right to make and administer its own laws. The state was above the religion and made it, above the gods and decreed their worship; and so it was but legal and natural that the emperor, as the head and symbol of the Roman state, should be declared divine, and that all men should be held bound to worship and believe as he determined and decreed.

Now, let us see how radically Christianity stood here opposed to all the old religions. It worked by persuasion, its great instrument was speech. It did not seek to live by the protection or help of the state, but wished to penetrate as truth and love the mind and heart of man. It did not ask the laws to favour it, asked only to be allowed to live and work in its own way. And so what is it we see when it first appears on the great stage of history? We see that it comes and appeals to reason, it speaks to intellect, it tries to persuade spirit. The man that goes out and preaches stands, where? On Mars Hill, and reasons with the philosophers. The man that goes to Corinth, does what? Preaches, and preaches that he may convert and change. It is as a power living by speech, living by persuasion, that Christianity begins to be. When it has persuaded, what does it require? That a man live a life holy unto God. Mark this, that where the old religions placed animal, the new religion placed spiritual sacrifices. Men were to offer their spirits, their bodies, their living souls unto God. Where the old religions placed outer service, the new religion placed purity, peace, faith, hope, love, service of kind. While the old religions stood in subordination to the state, the new stood in supremacy over man, was a moral law over him, and so over any society into which he might be gathered. All was changed, and every man it reached became a great factor of change, a means of making a new humanity, a whole world new.

II

1. Well, now, passing from these distinctive notes or features of the new religion, I would notice two of the ways in which the old Pagan and Jewish ideas affected and changed it. The first of these was the way in which the old sacerdotal ideas came back. Remember, it is one thing for a truth to be revealed, another thing for it to be understood. It takes

centuries before the mind of man grasps the meaning of a great truth. It takes centuries more before he is able to express it in outward action. Consider the situation; for ages the world had been accustomed to religions with priests, with sacrifices, with temples. The Jews had a priesthood, a temple, a ritual at once extensive and minute; all the Pagans had the same. Now when they came to think of Christianity, even after they had become Christian, the old elements in their minds were in some respects stronger than the new. They could not easily conceive a religion without those modes and orders which had seemed the very essence of all the religions they knew, and so they proceeded, though all unconsciously, to translate the new back into the old. And so they thought of the apostle, of the prophet, or the presbyter as a priest; and they could not think of a priest without thinking of a sacrifice, and they could not think of a sacrifice without thinking of a temple; and so old Pagan ideas came back and held, for many a drear century, sway within the Christian Church.

It is not possible here either to trace the history of the change or fully explain its nature and effects. But let us try to weigh a fact or two. In the earliest Christian literature, apostolic and post-apostolic, no man who bears office in the church is called a priest. In it there was no official priesthood, and none of the signs and rites associated with one. The men who held office were called either apostles, or prophets, or evangelists, or pastors, or teachers, or elders, or ministers, or overseers, but never priests. About the end of the second century, however, that fateful name begins to appear. A great Latin father, Tertullian, speaks of "the sacerdotal order," and calls the bishop priest, and even high priest, though he was far enough from allowing priesthood in any sense that denied the spiritual priesthood of universal Christian men. Half a century later another writer, Cyprian, makes quite a strong claim on behalf of an official priesthood, and shows us just beginning the change of the Lord's Supper from a simple feast of love and remembrance into a sacrificial ceremony. Now, once a change like this begins it proceeds rapidly, and the further it proceeds the more disastrous it becomes. It forced into Christianity many of the limitations and much of the materialism of Judaism and paganism. In the apostolic days every Christian man was a priest, with the right to approach God when and where he pleased; but this neo-heathenism tended to give, and ultimately gave, the official priest the right to stand between God and man, distributing the grace of the one, granting or denying access or pardon to the other. In the religion of Christ, no place was sacred or necessary to the worship of the Father, the one thing needful was the pure and true spirit; but the renascent sacerdotalism created a whole new order of sacred persons, places, ceremonies, acts, which had to be respected if the worship was to be approved. The Christianity of the New Testament was a religion inward and spiritual, all its virtues were those of the believing, meek, true and loving spirit; but the Christianity of the priesthood and their church became outward and material, consisted in things the priesthood could prescribe and regulate, rather than the obedience commanded and approved of God. You will see at once how this affected the religion and modified its action. It was then as always, the truth of God had to wrestle with the ignorance and sin and imperfection of man. These cannot be expelled by mechanical forces, only by moral means, and the conquests of moral agencies are slow, but in the process the nature of man is uplifted and renewed. His nature affected the religion, but it more mightily affected his nature. What was of God prevailed.

2. Then there was a second class of influences which we may describe as political. Men, as accustomed to a great state and religion as bound up with it, thought that apart from the forms of the state it could not be. So the result was that both in East and West, the state and the church tended to draw nearer and nearer in political form and idea to each other. It was an ill moment when Constantine took over his idea of Pontifex Maximus into the church. The old emperor had been supreme priest, the new emperor in the new religion tried to become the same. That either gave to the church a master, or, by turning the church into an organized state, with its hierarchies and graded orders, created the political interests and ambitions which made the church try to be master over the state. In the East

the state remained master, and we see the result in Athanasius banished from his see at the fiat of an emperor, or recalled when the emperor so willed. Or we see it in the great Chrysostom, when he dared to rebuke the vice of an unclean or impure court, banished by Arcadius, a tool in the hands of the vengeful Eudoxia. In the West there was the opposite process, where the church, developing into a mighty state, became a mighty power, seeking to control in its own interest all the secular policies. It may have ofttimes stood on the side of order, nay, in its earliest days it almost always so stood. But so vast a departure from the old original idea made the religion less potent for good than in its pure and primitive days. Yet, in spite of the return of the old sacerdotal, of the old political or civil idea, Christian truth lived, Christian thought worked, and there distilled into society through the Christian Church great ameliorative principles which were operative for good.

III

Now this brings us to the point where we must consider the action, even as so qualified, of Christian ideas, truths, or beliefs, on the prosperity and happiness of man. And I am anxious that this should be considered in relation, simply and purely, to the great industrial and economical questions.

1. Well, then, I will ask you to consider as a first step the state of the world as regards its social and

economical condition when Christianity appeared. And I will take it at its most favourable point, as it existed in Rome. Now Rome was a great city, it was the mistress of the world; the tribute of all places flowed into it. The Roman was a sturdy and stern man, proud of his great history, vain of his eternal city, remembering his republican virtues, and glorying in his past. What, then, was the state of Rome, the highest point of ancient civilization, in the first century of the Christian era? Here I want working men to listen, for I wish to speak purely and simply from the standpoint of one who believes that economical, industrial, and social questions are questions of religion, and who wishes to regard them altogether as such. Well, the population of Rome, if we are to take Mommsen, the greatest of all its historians in recent times, as our authority, was, in the first century, 1,610,000. How was it composed? There were 10,000 senators and knights, 60,000 foreigners, 20,000 garrison, 320,000 free citizens, 300,000 women and children, and 900,000 slaves. Mark that:—about three-fifths of the population of Rome were slaves. That is one fact.

(*a*) Now consider how the slaves affected industrial and social economics. You will notice in the first place, that these slaves were the absolute property of the master; he could do with them as you can do at this moment with your dog. Nay, your dog has more rights than a Roman slave had.

For English law has grown so tender that it protects even the animal from the cruelty of man ; but Roman law did not so protect the slave. Take, for example, a case like that of Flaminius, who, when a gay young friend said he had never seen a man in the agonies of death, had a slave killed to show him what he wished. Or take the case of Pollio, who liked delicate lampreys, and fed them with his slaves. Or take cases such as that of Cato the elder dealing with his slaves as cattle, mere tools for the creation of wealth, to be broken or sold when useless. They were things, chattels, and no man who was a Roman citizen need care what happened to them.

(β) But now there is another and no less pertinent question, how did slavery affect labour? Well, you perceive all labour was done by slaves ; trade and labour were altogether in the hands of the wealthy, but in a peculiar way : the rich who owned the land, owned the slaves, and through their slaves conducted trade. We know well what the conflict between labour and capital means. Yes, and with us labour can often hold its own ; but there was no conflict between labour and capital then, for labour was capital, all slaves were capital, men that worked for the masters, and the owners reaped the profit. Many a man tilled his farm by slaves working chained in gangs. Many a man conducted a vast business by slaves, who made the profit and handed it to him. Many a man produced the raw material, manufactured it, carried it, and sold it—all by means of his slaves ;

theirs being the labour, and his the reward. And the scale on which the richest Romans could do business of this kind may be judged from the fact that some had as many as 10,000 slaves, and even 20,000 was not an unknown number. The work, then, of the Capital was done by these 900,000 slaves, and so the wealth of Rome was gathered into the hands of the few thousand men who owned them ; and everywhere, except for these few thousand men, there was deep poverty, and within the poverty there was a slavery of a deeper and darker kind still

(γ) But there is a third question, which has an even more significant light to shed on the temper and state of the time. Whence came the supply of slaves? Rome could not of herself have produced and maintained so extraordinary a number; they were in large part the fruits of conquest. I said the tribute of the world flowed into Rome, and slaves were the tribute of the vanquished. If a Roman army conquered a province, or defeated another army, the captives, if they were not butchered in cold blood, were sent to Rome, to be sold as slaves. And here let me ask, and then leave you to answer, a simple question, yet one of profoundest moral import :—" Is it possible to calculate the degree in which this way of handling the conquered must have depraved the conquerors ? "

2. But now we must study the social and ethical effects of this system. How did the multitude of slaves affect the 320,000 free citizens? Where

work, labour, trade, was the mark and sign of bondage, with these no freeman could soil his hands. He could not labour, labour was a thing for slaves, and slaves alone. And so these 320,000 were idle, or they were worse than idle, the pimps, the buffoons, the men that lived to cater by crime for the pleasures of those who could afford to buy. But as a necessary consequence, when productive industry was so little cultivated, the citizens who despised labour had to be maintained by the emperor at the public expense. The feeding of these citizens was a great problem. The grain ships from all the provinces came to Rome, and every citizen had his right to so much grain, and, as a rule, rich or poor took it. How many of you that could earn your bread would take help raised by a poor-tax, in a word, parochial relief? What man, earning a good salary, would be so mean as to go and get his parochial allowance? Yet what was parochial allowance in its very worst form was taken by almost every man of these Roman citizens. And this dependency of the citizen on the government vitiated both, as this may illustrate : whenever an emperor came to power, or any fortunate event happened, he had to distribute great largesses ; he sat in his seat, he remained emperor only by keeping the multitude sweet and well-inclined to him, and they were well-inclined only when paid, and well paid ; and they often transferred their allegiance from the man that paid ill to the man that paid well. And so a Nero, and a Domitian, and a Caligula could reign, though each was shameful to his kind, because they not only were supported by the legionaries, but condescended to pay well the citizens who were too proud to work, but not too proud to live as beggarly dependants on an evil emperor.

But there were other and no less inevitable results. If you wish to keep a people sweet, you must not only feed them; if they have no work to do you must amuse them, and the amusing is the harder and more arduous thing. And how did the great Roman emperors amuse their men? Why, they built splendid amphitheatres in every Roman city, most of all in imperial Rome. There the ruins may still be viewed. Look at that mighty Colosseum, capable of seating 87,000 people. Think what it means. It means that an emperor had a people so idle, that he not only had to maintain them, but to amuse them. And what were the amusements? Whole rows of gladiators, men, or even ungentle women, met there, with knife, shield, and sword, to fight, row upon row, and unto death. And ofttimes, when the weaker went down, he might look his look of pity that cried for mercy. But there, in the crowded benches, the empress and many another dainty dame would put down their thumbs, which meant, "No mercy; do him to death!" And if they did not fight man to man, then they fought man and beast, lion, tiger, bear, sometimes the man defenceless, sometimes the man with offensive weapons. In a show, given by wise Julius Cæsar, 320 pairs of gladiators fought;

Titus, the good and gracious, held a series of shows which extended over one hundred days; Trajan, the just, celebrated a triumph by an exhibition in which 5000 contended; Domitian excelled himself and discovered a new sensation by instituting a fight between dwarfs and women. There was a people glutted with blood, fed with slaughter, amused with death! And it is told that it became a kind of study in certain cases to watch the lines on the face of the dying. That was a nice and refined æstheticism, yet the most fit for the spectators of the gladiatorial show!

Such was Rome, and Rome in the early years of our Christian era, Rome in its refinement, Rome in its pride, Rome in its might. And if the Romans were not careful for toil and labour, or careful for life, what cared they for the defenceless? Infants are a joy to man; childhood is sweet and beautiful to us; yet in Rome what so common as exposure? what so little deemed a crime? what so little punished as an offence? Nay, men followed as a trade taking up the exposed children that they might turn them to the basest of uses, that they might make them live the most miserable of lives. Do you think the ancient world happy, radiant, because undarkened by the shadow of the cross? You can only so think in your ignorance. Its good was all for the few, the rich and the strong; but for the masses, the mighty multitudes of the poor and the conquered, the dependent and the enslaved, it was a miserable world, and their lot a lot of misery. The very sense of their rights was not yet born; the feeling of obligation towards them waited on the footsteps of Christ.

IV

Now into this world, and face to face with it, Christianity came; and how did the religion affect the world? It is easy for us to see how truth must act; truth needs to work slowly, with many a great and painful struggle, into mind, and through mind into life. We think that a man has just to believe in order to be a new man. But though he is a new man, it is long ere the new manhood becomes perfect in its blossom, longer still ere the new man makes a new humanity; and so we must watch the slow, yet sure and most effective way in which Christianity, in its grand ideal period, went to work. Let me sketch in rapid outline one or two of the branches of its action.

First, slavery. It could not and it did not abolish slavery; yet it declared itself in its ideal period the foe of slavery. In Christ there is neither Jew nor Greek, bond nor free. In the church there was no slave and no master; there all were servants of Christ, and members one of another. Slowly, as Christianity prevailed, the idea of man's equality entered into the heart of society. When you come to Justinian and his laws, slavery is still allowed, but to kill a slave is made a crime. Over him Christian law throws its shield. When you come later down still, the slave gains new rights. He can become a free man, he can enter into a religious order, he can there become the peer of the best, and in the new states that Christianity formed slavery, in the old sense, had no place. Nay, in spite of its many sins and imperfections, look how the church welded in Spain Iberian and Visigoth together; how in France it welded Kelt and Frank; how in England it welded first Briton and Saxon, then Saxon and Norman, creating an entirely new ideal, the ideal of a society without slaves, wheremanhood is known and honoured, and has its rights confessed.

Then, secondly, let us see how it affected the feelings and spirit of humanity. One of the earliest decrees of the Emperor Constantine was against the amphitheatre. The people passionately loved and still clung to their brutal play. But Christian faith held on against it, till finally, in the reign of Honorius, when a great victory was being celebrated, the monk Telemachus leaped into the ring, and gave himself a prey to the wild beasts. While many an angry howl rose against the man who had spoiled their sport, it was found that his deed had given the death-blow to the great evil; for the consciences of men were pricked and touched by that act of self-sacrifice. Then the great arena had its doom, the public conscience ratified the imperial decree, and the amphitheatre ceased.

Then, thirdly, with the greater love of freedom and the softer social spirit, there came a large belief in the dignity of labour. Jesus had been a worker, Paul had been a worker, John and Peter and all the apostles had been workers. They gave dignity to toil. The Roman citizen could not soil his hands; the Christian preacher worked, toiling with his hands. And so labour became dignified, was made honourable; men found that no manhood was so base as an idle manhood, manhood that loved to be relieved from toil and work. And now mark that this went on even when you little think it. The idle monks are frequently blamed; yet the monasteries used to be scenes of toil. You often go to Bolton or to Fountains, and you say in the wise manner of to-day, " Those old monks knew what they were doing; they placed their houses in favoured spots, they chose beautiful situations." Yet they found them deserts, and they made them gardens; they found them moors, and they planted them, and drained them, and made them fertile fields. Our agriculture, our culture, our learning, owes more to the monasteries than many a modern man thinks. They made, or helped to make, work religious. " Laborare est orare," they said; to work is to worship, to toil is to pray.

Then, fourthly, see how the Christian religion consecrated the home. It threw over the woman, it threw over the child, the halo of a great love. The child was of the kingdom of heaven. He who gave our faith its being was born of a woman, and so made woman sacred. I confess that there are moments when, with all my strong dislike to priest-craft, sacerdotalism, and the poor and external form of Christianity it implies, I can feel how it taught us reverence for woman ; how its adoration of a woman helped to create the purer, the nobler ideal of the home, the purer and grander faith in maternity. The man who is capable of despising his mother, of disowning or neglecting a wife, or being cruel to a child, is no man, he wants the soul of chivalry. The faith that brought out that great latent passion in man for gentleness to woman and child, has achieved a right noble work, has done a grand thing.

But, fifthly, besides the consecration of the home, the early church organized the charities, the beneficences of time. You know not how destitute of true and generous action the ancient world was ! It was a new thing that Lucian laughed at,—the sight of Christians visiting the prisons and ministering to the captives. He thought them simpletons, weak people who offered themselves as easy prey to the designing and crafty. He did not know that their act expressed a new passion, the enthusiasm of humanity, and had in it the promise of redemption for the world. It was a new thing, despised of many a man, to see poverty relieved, to see disease nursed, to see pestilence faced. If time had permitted I could have told how, when the barbarian hordes swept over Italy or across Africa or into Spain, rich Pagans fled far into their retreats, and left pestilence and famine and death to rage as they listed. But brave men like Ambrose and Augustine, faced the desolation and death. The matrons and the maids of the new faith went out to nurse in hospitals, in churches, by many a bedside, creating, where only misery had been, a sweet and gentle peace. The religion of Christ created charity; at its very birth it stood forth to organize the beneficence of man into the instrument of the providence of God.

But above all, and most of all, what Christianity in these centuries did was to substitute a new mental, a new moral, a new spiritual basis for life. Life was made far sweeter, far nobler, far diviner by having a grander basis. No imperial decree, no fiat of state, no word of mere might constituted the organizing force of society. Men believed in a living God who was Eternal Sovereign and Father, in a living Christ who was an Eternal Brother. Men believed that man was to man a brother the world over. As brothers they owed duties that time could never fulfil, that place could never separate. The faith, however imperfect its forms, that lived and worked for these sublime and glorious ends, was a faith that indeed came from God, and made preparation and provision for another and better time when the large and eternal principles of righteousness could be applied to life and society.

V

THE CHRISTIAN RELIGION IN MODERN EUROPE

THE point we have reached is one of the deepest interest. It brings us face to face with questions that relate to the immediate past, and concern the living present. Ancient history is the field of the special student. He works in it, knows it, loves it, lives in it, is perhaps more at home with its persons, principles, events than with the men, the problems, and the interests that appear and wrestle, that prevail and vanish on the stage of the passing hour. But modern Europe is our own very world. We belong to it, breathe its atmosphere, live its life, and think its thoughts, and feel its electric currents thrill along our nerves. Its every movement is answered by the responsive pulsations of our hearts. Now this modern world of ours, in which we live, is one full of good, yet full also of evil; wealthier than any past age, freer, better educated, more informed, with vaster energies exercised on the field of politics, commerce, industry, science, literature, art, and religion. But it is also a world that in the lucid moments that come between the periods of its possession by the pride of knowledge, feels, as no other age ever felt, over-burdened by a sense of its poverty, misery, failure, vice, and crime. There are in our world more and mightier forces contending against evil, than in any previous time. They fight all along the line a victorious battle. But while so fighting, never was age so moved and so possessed with the consciousness of evil. Now the sense of suffering is one thing, the actual amount and degree of suffering another, and altogether different. The conditions of happiness are to-day more and higher than ever in the history of the world before. But then the feeling of unhappiness is perhaps deeper, the sense of it keener and more real. Yet is not that an element of the highest promise of good? Evils that men do not feel, they will not remedy; evils that are deeply felt are evils not to be borne: and where they are not to be borne, they are certain to be abolished. To make an age conscious of evil is the first condition of making it consciously happy, in preparing it for larger happiness. There is at this moment a wide sense of suffering and of sin, but then within it there is also a great faith, a faith that we can win, and that we shall win, the saner, the more normal state of happy holy being. Modern Europe is far more conscious of suffering than ancient Europe, but in that consciousness there live and work the elements that have the most promise of deliverance, those that look toward the great and permanent ameliorative state that is sure to come.

I

1. Now, in attempting to discuss so large a question as Christianity in modern Europe, it is easy to see that there is a great variety of sides from which it can be discussed, while only a few from which it is possible to discuss it here and now. We might look at the question as a question of Churches. That indeed would be a matter of profoundest interest and instruction. We could compare the Greek, the Roman, the Reformed, the Lutheran, the Anglican, the multitudinous Free Churches of the modern world; describe their respective characters, the number of adherents they possess, the truths or doctrines they hold, the constitutions they boast, the work they have done or tried to do, the influence they have exercised or still exercise. That were indeed a noble as well as an instructive work. The churches represent perhaps the mightiest mass of devoted labour, of noble living, of ungrudging service of our kind, ever at any moment seen in the history of man. I put it to every fair-minded person as a simple problem: imagine all the Churches with their agencies and institutions suddenly destroyed, can you conceive the result for our order, for our society and age? Think—would not the myriad-branched stream of charity be almost completely dried up at its source? Would not the ministries of mercy, of

healing, of gentleness, of readiness to rescue the fallen, and cure the diseased, be suddenly brought to an end? Would not the inspiration that lifts many a life out of the dust be extinguished, and some of the fairest and most beautiful phases of human character be utterly blighted and blurred? I know that in certain places what professes to be satire, but is only brutal coarseness, delights to magnify the individual error, crime, or sin of men who are held to represent Christian Churches and the Christian religion. That shallow system which does not or will not see the nobility, the magnanimity, the heroism that in many a life serves its kind without money and without price, is no system conscious of its own truth, fighting a noble battle with noble weapons. Men and women! a cause that needs an ignoble instrument is an ignoble cause. Fear not to say, the cause that can see nothing to honour in religion, when it has created and is creating millions of honourable lives, is no cause that believes in its own truth, or can wield a power for righteousness.

It would be easy, too, by comparing the churches of to-day with the mediæval churches to show how much mightier the former are. The ages of faith are now, not once were. The age of ignorance and superstition, or ceremony, lies behind, in mediæval bygone Christianity. The age of faith is in our midst. True, you may think of a time when all over Europe one church reigned, when the monastery was as many acred—acred up to the lip, consolled up to the chin

—as the modern peer. You may think of the time when out of their vast wealth the monks built their stately buildings, or the church reared its grand cathedral, as a time of faith. I think otherwise, and turn from then to now. I think of a land like England, where men often out of their poverty maintain and propagate their faith. I have known many a one who has given up large prospects of commercial wealth, large prospects of professional success, and lived a life of purest poverty that he might live a life altogether unto Christ. Or I think of lands like that lying beyond the Atlantic, where all churches are free, and a living people make the living church. And I say, look how the fact stands: The man in the market, on the exchange, in the factory, in the infirmary, by the sick bed, anywhere, everywhere, whose life is possessed and ruled and inspired by the great truths of religion, is the true measure of its power. And never at any moment in the whole history of the Christian faith were there so many men filled, commanded, guided, by the holier and simpler truths of our faith.

2. Yet we must look at the matter not simply as a question of Churches or Christian living, but also as a matter of belief. Here I will say, never was age more marked by its strong and victorious belief than ours. I know what I say. The truth of Christ is slowly subduing the mind of man into itself. Never was His authority so great as it is now. It is greater now than in that mediæval time, when religion was

the great concern of the few, the mere pastime of the many. Then indeed the penances, the absolutions, the festivals, the fasts, the indulgences granted by a mighty priesthood helped the Church often only to gain influence over men by making a league with sin. It is now mightier than in the Reformation time, when princes and statesmen, ecclesiastics and divines made it their exclusive business, and armies fought to determine to what Church or to what creed the whole country or the whole people should belong. It is mightier, too, than in an age like the eighteenth century, the pre-eminent age of apologetics. Then it was that on the one side there stood men like Toland, Collins, and Tindal, Bolingbroke and Chubb and Hume: and on the other men like Butler, and Berkeley, and Paley. Yet great as were the apologies of that time, the greatest apologist of them all had to confess, "I know not how it has happened, but so it is, that many take for granted that the Christian religion is not so much as a subject of inquiry, but is at length discovered to be fictitious." That may not now be said. This century has given to faith its brightest sons. The men who when it is past will stand up as the great time-marks of the period, are men who boast of strong and noble faith. The thinkers that have had the mightiest influence are Christian thinkers. It may be that we have phases and forms of loud-speaking infidelity. It is true, nevertheless, that we have a great deep strong "sea of faith," a sea of faith that never was so near its full. And still it will continue to rise. As man's knowledge extends, so will it enlarge. It is not knowledge that religion has to fear, it is ignorance : it is the absence of science applied to religion. Give us more scientific spirit, give us wider knowledge, give us calm impartial study of man and man's past and man's spirit : and religion will reign, its power will grow, its might increase.

Now these are phases of our question and subject that might fitly enough be here and now discussed. But they are not the peculiar phases that I wish to present to you. I have invited working men : to working men as workers I wish to speak. I have tried to exhibit religion in relation to history, to society, to the great practical problems that emerge in connexion with man in his social and collective life ; and to that phase I am pre-eminently wishful to adhere. I want to look at Christianity—the Christian religion in modern Europe—as it has affected the political, the social, the economical questions ; or rather the great principles that lie as the common basis underneath them all. And we look at these aspects and phases only in order that we may discover what religion is, and that we may say what it is to men who are workers and toilers, anxious to find freedom in the world, anxious to find wealth, character, happiness, and to know that to him that worketh there are proper wages and sure reward.

II

1. Such, then, being our peculiar problem, I would say, at the outset, that modern Europe, as distinguished from ancient Europe, may be traced back into two great movements; a movement of the fifteenth century, and a movement of the sixteenth; one the Renaissance, the other the Reformation. The Renaissance affected and affects art and letters. The Reformation affected and affects religion. The Renaissance was the revival of letters, touched all questions that related to man as a thinking, perceiving, living being, who needs to be educated. The particular form that it took was in great part due to the rise of the Turkish power in the East, and the consequent extinction of the Greek Empire. At its fall many Greeks travelled westward bringing their language, their ancient literature, the laws, the practically lost knowledge of Greece and Rome. Their main home and centre of work was Italy. There they taught many a joyous and earnest spirit to read Plato, to know Aristotle, to discourse with the ancient orators and feel the exaltation and inspiration of the great poets. There men who had been accustomed to a mediæval and often heathenish Christianity, suddenly found themselves face to face with the old paganism, pure and simple. And it became as it were the basis of their lives. They went back to the old naturalism, the love of flesh and of nature that

had so marked, especially in its decadence, the ancient world.

Now how did this pagan revival, which replaced in great part mediæval Christianity, affect these cities of Italy? It found them free : Florence rich, artistic, strong, rejoicing in its political freedom and republican institutions : Pisa enterprising, its rival, almost its equal : Bologna, Padua, full of life, the one studying law, the other studying medicine, both great in their universities : Genoa, Venice, both queens of the sea, sending their fleets afar, bringing in the riches of distant Asia, making their merchant princes prouder than any royal blood in Europe : all free, all energetic, as it were in the flood tide of victorious life. But in the presence of that revived paganism, enervating public life at its source, what happened? The rise of the Medici at Florence, the usurpations of tyranny and the growth of a pernicious luxury in them all, made these Italian cities—once the freest, the wealthiest, and most enterprising of Europe—the poorest and most reactionary. There Italy remains, the victim of two great forces, the Renaissance in its classic naturalism and the Church it tried to supersede. Most beautiful, most historic of European countries, she lives at this day only in the first energies of a new attempt at life, seeking to catch up the other and more northern nations which have sped far forward in the great path of progress opened by freedom.

2. The Renaissance as it passed into the Reformation was by it incorporated and made a servant, true

and good, of religion, helping the discovery and the knowledge of the old religious books. But taking the Reformation simply by itself, we find it was an attempt to recover the lost or forgotten ideal of the Christian religion, an attempt to return to the real and genuine religion of Christ. As indicated in the previous lecture, two great heathen influences had entered the Church. The first was sacerdotal, the second political. The sacerdotal brought into a religion which knew no priest, no temple, no sacrifice save what was spiritual, an immense hierarchy, a disciplined and organized priesthood, that by command of the access to God and the rewards and penalties of the life to come, had become an organized tyranny, which tyrannized not through what it got from Christ, but only through what it acquired from Judaized heathenism. The sacerdotal mind and practice is invariably disastrous to spiritual religion. The man who stands where only Christ should stand, between man and God, obscures faith, hides God behind his office and his rites. Where God cannot be seen for a man, the man conceals God, and in so doing is the great enemy of man. But while the sacerdotal was mischievous on the one side, the political was mischievous on the other. It made the Church aim at a supremacy over the State, which was not spiritual and moral, but political and secular; a supremacy which consisted, not in the reign of beliefs and ideals through the reason over the conscience, but in one organized polity commanding all the rest. The distinctive element of the Christian religion had been the reign of God in the human soul, commanding the man by commanding the man's spirit and conscience. When the Church was taken and organized into the great *civitas*, or State, or polity which sought to win, by its command over the future, authority in the present, in all that pertained to civil as well as religious life—it perverted Christianity and turned it back into the older heathenism. Now the Reformation was a great attempt to escape from these two Pagan elements, to get back into a purer and nobler, because a more primitive religion. It meant to say, not the religion of the Church but the religion of Christ is what man needs.

So Luther said, "Get quit of the Pope, get rid of the priests, rid of all that stands between the individual soul and God. Let God and the soul stand face to face. Let God and the soul know and be known to each other. Here, in this immediate knowledge of God given by God, I stand ; I can do no other. God help me, for God commands me." His watchword, which summed up this belief, was "Justification by faith,"—faith, face to face knowledge of God, and justification, peace in the conscience where God lived, where God's voice was heard, believed, obeyed. That cry wakened Germany. They say, Luther made the literature of Germany. Do you know what that means ? To make a literature means to make the mind of the people. To create the literature of a people is to create a people's spirit, its thought, its science, its whole inmost life; and, his enemies being witness, Luther did that; he created the literature of Germany by that word of his, by his revival of the old faith. It entered into the spirit of Teutonic man and made his thought anew.

III

That was only one section of the Reformation; there was another. Calvin went further than Luther. He not only insisted on God and man standing face to face, but he insisted on applying his notion of religion by building it into a state. Now I do not mean either to defend or expound Calvin's notion of God, any more than I intend to defend and expound his attempted realization of a State. I think both had august and noble elements. I think both had very terrible, very stern, very awful elements indeed. One thing I mean you to see and so must emphasize in your hearing: wherein he found faith he found life, he made belief into a law for living: he made the duty of the conscience to God the foremost duty of man. This conception of human duty he so bound up with his notion of God, his idea of religion, as to compel unity to enter into the life of the real believer. So doing, Calvin powerfully affected five countries—Switzerland, France, Holland, England, Scotland.

1. Switzerland we may leave aside. But look at France. There came to her reformed people the hardest problem that could be set to any one. The

faith they held, their king would not allow. The duty their conscience demanded, the State declared a duty not to be permitted. It is hard to be obedient citizens when the first law of the State contradicts the first necessity of conscience. Yet this people, though they stood for God against their king, became, whenever opportunity allowed, industrious, peaceable citizens, making their cities beautiful, their districts wealthy. When inspired by influences born not of religion simply, but of other and baser motives as well, Louis XIV. revoked the edict that allowed them to live in peace, they bade, in great numbers, farewell to their Fatherland, that they might go elsewhere and serve their God. And so there came this principle through them : Religion is so supreme a matter of conscience, that the State which means to remain one, united, compact, harmonious, must grant freedom in religion. Martyrs to the doctrine they were ; but in the State as in the Church, the blood of the martyr is the seed of freedom, power, and success.

2. Note, next, the influence in Holland. Holland you know has a noble history. The king it had for ruler, Philip of Spain,—forsooth no good man in the moral sense, though most pious in the ecclesiastical,—held that his subjects must be of his faith. But these Dutchmen said, " This light of the reformed religion has come to us from God. We believe it to be His truth, and we shall obey God, rather than King Philip." Patient they had been,

calm, industrious, fighting that great fight of theirs against the tides of old Ocean in the swamps by the sea. They had built out the waves; beneath their level they had cultivated their fields. A peaceful but most enduring people they were, to whom religion, as now understood, came, a very revelation of the presence and power of God. They mustered in their cities and mustered in their fields; and against them came the great legions of Spain, led by Parma, led by Alva, led by Don John of Austria, led by the most famous captains of the age. But these men of Holland stood by their cities and fought in their swamps like heroes. They let the sea sweep over their fields and waste their cities, rather than yield the freedom that came to them from God And when they had beaten back the mighty power of Spain, and gained their freedom, they nobly showed how a people that had fought to the death for their own freedom could help to make other peoples free. Their land became the very home and house of refuge for the oppressed of all lands. There freedom of thought and speech did reign, and reign in peace.

3. Next in England. The Anglican Church is very proud of not being a Puritan Church, reformed by means of Puritan theology. Yet the great English people lie under immensest obligations to Calvin, to Geneva, to the reformed men and doctrine. The men Calvin influenced were called Puritan, which meant—they thought religious men were men who ought to be pure, holy, of good report. These Puritan

men became lovers of freedom, and they won freedom for you. When men said of a man weak, self-willed, proud, very much in want of all that makes manhood true and generous, " He is king by Divine right, sits enthroned to be obeyed as the very vicar and representative of God," these Puritans stood forward and answered, " Nay, this people of England is a free people. We stand under obligation to God first. We are bound to obey Him. Being bound to obey Him, when the king commands what conflicts with the command of God, we must obey God rather than the king." Believing that, they fought their fight, and they won it, even though it seemed in defeat. Charles I., when he lost his head, made this great principle manifest and intelligible to all kings, that they are for peoples, and not peoples for them. That is the political principle England owed to her Puritans, and to the fundamental article of their faith ; the article that, religion being of God, the religious man can be responsible for his faith, and for the conduct his faith demands, to God alone.

Nor was their contribution to freedom limited to England. The revolution they accomplished not without blood, made the bloodless revolution of a later generation possible ; and supplied at once principles and inspirations that were in the succeeding centuries to help oppressed and impoverished peoples to cast off the regal and sacerdotal tyrannies under which they groaned. And they did more than teach ; they sent out a branch that was destined to bear the noblest fruits of freedom. Of these Puritans many finding it hopeless to expect to be allowed to live at home and serve God in their own way, crossed the ocean and made another English nation beyond the sea. And they took with them the principles that lie at the foundation of the great American Republic, principles which have secured absolute freedom of religious thought, and made our kin beyond the sea the freest of all the peoples earth has known.

4. Lastly, in Scotland. What did the reformed faith find there, and what did it accomplish? It found a people barbarous, downtrodden, enslaved, made coarse and brutal by a long war of independence against their mighty neighbour; and as it were by the breath of a creative word, it made that people stand up happy, free, educated, strong. Whatever success the sons of that land have achieved, they have achieved by the faith, and the political energy created of the faith, they received from the reformed religion.

IV

Now this rapid historical sketch has showed us that the Reformation, by virtue of its being a return, or an attempted return, to the religion of Christ, the purer and more genuine Christian religion, accomplished far more than it attempted. It revealed ideas, energies, elements in religion that worked powerfully for human freedom, that created in the State a freer and a higher life, and created in man and in society nobler purpose, greater independence, that love of equal freedom and equal justice which but expresses the love of man. The principles that thence emerge may be illustrated on one or two points of detail. That their action may be apprehended, we must come down to matters of living interest, matters of clear historical certainty that ought to be familiar to you.

1. Now, let me ask you as men who work, what are the three great terms that you think, as it were, the true Palladia of the order most to be desired? They are the terms which were the watchwords of the French Revolution—Liberty, Equality, Fraternity. I cannot enter into a discussion as to the French Revolution. It has two phases, and can only be understood when both these are regarded. One phase is its negative, the other its positive side. Its negative phase it owes to Voltaire, to Rousseau, to the Encyclopædists, and owes it to them mainly because of the great abuses against which they had to contend. The French Revolution was a supreme act of retribution, the supreme act of national retribution on the stage of modern history. Under and after Louis XIV., the king and the Church had bound themselves in an unholy alliance. That alliance meant bondage to man, meant poverty to the multitude, meant abdication of the highest political and social duties both of king and Church. The revolution, in its negative phase, hastened, though not caused, by the literature which exposed the unholy alliance, was an act of

retribution, and retribution was never more deserved and never more inevitable. On the positive side it was an affirmation of principles which did not come from these negative quarters. It was the affirmation of the principles of Liberty, Equality, and Fraternity; although in its practical working-out it was the greatest affront to these principles, and repudiation of them which modern times have known. I am concerned purely with the great positive principles, not with the event, not with the method in which it was conducted, not with its retributive relation to the past, but only with its relation to these three great ideas of Liberty, Equality, Fraternity—whence came they?

i. Liberty. Liberty is of two kinds, political and religious. Political liberty is revealed in the highest and most perfect degree where the people have the right absolute to make and to amend their own laws. Religious liberty is realized where every citizen possesses the right to judge in religious matters, and to determine the faith or the religion by or after which he shall order his life. Whence came the two great ideas as now understood, liberty, political and religious?

(*a*) Political. It did not come from antiquity. No Oriental monarchy possessed or possesses it. They, every one, were or are despotic. It did not come from any ancient European state. You had a slight glimpse of what Rome was; there three-fifths of the population were slaves, and only two-fifths free. But there is Greece, and you will say,

"Think of those great republics of Greece; at Athens, where Plato lived, and Aeschulos sang; at Lacedaemon, where dwelt the great heroes of Grecian story? Think of those happy times before the Peloponnesian war—the days of the heroes of Marathon and Thermopylæ, when Attica and Sparta were free!" But what do you mean by free? How many made the State? Hear this: There were for every twenty-seven freemen in Attica a hundred slaves, almost four slaves to one free man : *that* was the ancient ideal of liberty!

When you come to modern times and ask, "Whence came our liberty? Has it come from free thought?" Let us appeal to history; its testimony no man can gainsay. Who is the father of modern materialism? Thomas Hobbes. And what says he? The primitive state was a state of war, the strongest man—and this is modern Evolution—prevailed, and so became king: might is right; and the king, being king by divine might, he alone is the free man, other men are bound to be his servants and do his will. But, you say, remember the later freethinkers! Well, try Bolingbroke; he believes in a patriot king, and sketched the ideal of one. And what sort of king was he? One who by skilful manipulation of the people was able to win, retain, and exercise absolute power, using all their political institutions as instruments of his will, deluding them by a representation that was only a means to his own ends. But a still more typical man is

David Hume, the choicest sceptic Europe has ever known. Hume had two great enemies, and he loved nothing better than to swoop down first on one and then on the other. And these two great enemies of his were religion and liberty. Try Edward Gibbon. No man ever clothed a sneer in language so stately, or mocked in periods so majestic. Well, then, in the correspondence that unbosoms his inmost convictions, he warns his friend against the Anti-Slavery Agitation, for wild ideas of the rights and natural equality of men lurk in it. Democracy he hates; to him it is the last apostasy. He has only scorn for it: and he speaks of the French Revolution as an accursed thing. But these, you will say, are old, even antiquated men; try, then, so late an exponent of freethought as Comte. Where does he find his ideal king? Not in the sovereign of England; not in the monarch of any Constitutional State; but in the Czar, the Emperor of all the Russias, the greatest of the autocrats, Nicholas. No, if you want political freedom, it is to States that have known what it was to believe in the Christian religion that you must go. You must go to Holland, as she issues purified from her baptism of blood, strengthened in her faith, and ennobled in her spirit by the unequal, yet victorious struggle against Spain. You must go to England as the Puritans made her. You must go to Scotland as she was made by Knox. You must go to America, so largely formed, organized, and governed by the sturdy Puritan men of New England and the mild inflexible Friends and stalwart Presbyterians of Pennsylvania. And underneath all you find that the grand dominant factors are the religious ideas, the faith that came through Jesus Christ.

(β) But, perhaps, some of you will tell me that with religious liberty it is different. On the contrary, I tell you that with religious liberty the same truth holds in a still more eminent degree. Gibbon, in many a memorable phrase, stated his faith that the Old World was tolerant. Yes, it was tolerant—to gentlemen of culture, to persons of refined taste, who could, while taking part in religious services, despise religion; but never tolerant to an earnest man, who dared openly to differ from the religion of the State. I love Plato; I look upon his books every day, and I never look upon them but with love. The thoughts that lived in him are living thoughts in many a mind still. But now look at his idea of religious freedom. Hypocrisy he would punish as a crime. Disloyalty to the gods accepted by the State, he would visit with imprisonment, solitary and stern, for five years, and if the man at the end still rebelled, he would have him given over to death. That was the idea of perhaps the most enlightened man in all antiquity. And, as we have already seen, it was the same in Rome. There the laws of the State and public opinion were just as severe in dealing with men who had broken with the ancient faith, or had dared to accept a new one To this the early Christian persecutions alone were a sufficient witness.

Where, then, do you find the first assertion of religious liberty? In the Fathers of the Christian Church. Tertullian, for example, says, "It is ill homage to God to compel a man to serve him, as if He could be pleased with the service of hypocrisy." Athanasius says, "No forced obedience pleases God: He dislikes that men should be made religious by hatchet and by sword." Hilary of Poitiers told an Emperor, "You govern that all may enjoy sweet liberty; and peace can be established only by allowing each to live wholly according to his own convictions." "God is the Lord of the universe, and requires not an obedience that is forced." And Lactantius, one of the most eloquent of the Fathers, argued that only reason, never compulsion, availed in religion, which could be defended not by slaying, but by dying; not by wasting, but by suffering; not by injustice, but by fidelity.

When we come to modern times, what do we find? Now that the principle is gained, you get many a man who has denied religion crying, give us freedom of thought. But look at the men who have made the modern belief in liberty of mind, and do you find that they were anti-religious, atheistic, infidel? Here is Hobbes's principle: "The prince has a right to say what his subjects are to believe." So great is that right that if any subject dares to deny what the king enjoins, he commits a crime against the law of the State. If a man were to come from the Indies and teach his religion where another has been established, he ought to be prosecuted for crime. Nay, if the king be infidel, yet the people are to believe after his manner, for he was appointed to his office of God! Where God has appointed, men are bound to obey. So held and so reasoned the man who may be most justly termed the father and founder of modern Materialism.

Again, no man did more to bring round the French Revolution on the negative side than Rousseau. And what did he teach in his "Social Contract"? He lays down the natural articles of belief, and they are to be articles of citizenship. If a man denies them, he is to be exiled, exiled not as denying religious dogma, but because he is "unsocial," violates, as it were, one of the primary articles of association. If a man, who has confessed himself as "social," and thus expressed his "sociability," is unfaithful to the profession of belief that admitted to society, then he ought to die as guilty of crime against the law, the social law on which the society or state was based, and which he had accepted and received. In the "Spirit of Laws," Montesquieu, another precursor of the French Revolution, teaches, that where an established religion is, there no new religion ought to be allowed to be. An established religion is a law of the land, and no land, he argued, with fine contempt for the rights of conscience, can allow its laws to lie neglected. And grant the principles from which the men reasoned, and we must concede that these were legitimate inferences;—clear, plain, logical deductions from a system that posits, as the grand parent of social order, force, whether dubbed as matter, or social contract, or regal power, or indeed any form of unmoral might.

If, then, I want to find where religious freedom came from in modern times, where am I to go? Lecky says, "Toleration is created by scepticism, and belongs to a sceptical age." But all modern history disproves that assertion. Where religion is made a matter of conscience and not of the magistrate, toleration is necessary. Where religion is made no matter of the conscience, but of the magistrate, intolerance and persecution are inevitable. So we find those Reformers and religious thinkers of whom I have already spoken, men like Jacobs, like Hanserd Knollys, like John Robinson, maintaining—religion is a matter of conscience; therefore the magistrate ought to leave to conscience the question of religion, and in no way interfere with it. Roger Williams, having pleaded in England and in New England for toleration, realized religious freedom in his settlement on Narragansett Bay. Harry Vane, the younger, a stern and true, yet most devout and tender spirit, a typical Puritan and Republican, was also a great advocate of the same principle, with faith enough to put it in practice when he was in power. In these days, when I wish to brace my spirit, to feel the strength of a great conviction which fears no discussion, and lies open on all sides to the light, which it craves as God's own gift, where do I so gladly go as to the Areopagitica of John Milton? There, in that speech for unlicensed printing, stands forward the grandest plea for freedom of thought which the English language or any other language contains. Later, too, did not the "Letters on Toleration" by John Locke, reason out, on narrower and less noble grounds it is true, but still, on religious grounds, the same great principle? The only convincing and victorious plea for freedom of thought, for liberty to believe according to reason and speak according to conscience, is the one that finds its ultimate principle and basis in the great faith, that religion belongs to the man and to the man's God, that it is the sacred inmost possession of conscience, and must be free from the magistrate, a matter in which the responsibility is to God only.

When you go from the actual advocacy to the attempted realization of the principle, our position holds even more completely. Where, as a matter of historical fact, was religious freedom first realized by a state? In Holland. She had won freedom, had shaken off Spain, and had learned from her own bitter experience what freedom and religion meant. And so almost as soon as she had achieved liberty, she became the home of the persecuted in Europe. There, within the very country which had been quickened, revived, created by a great religious enthusiasm, religious freedom reigned. There you might find the French Descartes writing, pleading, free to speak as became the father of modern philosophy. There you might find Italian, Spanish, and Portuguese Jews, tolerated while intolerant. Spinoza, cast out by the synagogue, but tolerated by the reformed state, there stands forward to advocate his Pantheism and his political theory. There, too, you might discover English Puritans like Perkins and Ames, like Robinson and Jacobs, erecting their churches, addressing their flocks, free to speak the thing they willed. When the same principles were recognized in Rhode Island, by Roger Williams's settlement, in the settlement of Penn, and finally through all the states of the American Republic, it was done for religious reasons, in vindication of those rights conscience most strongly affirms when it most strenuously believes that God is its only Sovereign, and that where He reigns no man or magistrate can be allowed to interfere.

But when Revolution in France passed into the hands of Deists and Atheists, what happened? Ay, *what* happened? I do not simply refer to the way in which the Church was, so to speak, levelled to the dust, and the clergy expelled or sent to the guillotine. I refer to such events as the guillotining of Clootz and Chaumette. The deistic, the Worship-of-the-Supreme-Being, party said, " These men are atheists: they deny the immortality of the soul, a doctrine which comforted Socrates in his death: the idea of the Supreme Being and the immortality of the soul is a continual appeal to justice; it is, therefore, social and republican, and so the men who deny it ought to die." And on this very ground, maintained and vindicated by Robespierre, nineteen of the worship-of Reason and deity-of-the-people party, including "Anaxagoras" Chaumette, "Anacharsis" Clootz, and Hébert, were doomed to death, sacrifices to their own principle—" There is now one god only, the people." And even they themselves, Hébert and Chaumette and Clootz, the men of the atheistic party, were no better. To utter the word Providence was denounced as a crime, and to publish a book that expressed belief in God was declared a crime the law ought to punish and prevent. And to-day, if you want to find a party that has in its heart the will to be intolerant, you have but to look across the Channel, and there you will find the party that is most aggressively negative prepared to proceed to the extremest measures of repression, both as regards the profession and practice of religion. Political liberty, liberty of thought in matters religious, was made by the religion of Christ, especially as it existed before it was civilly established and after it was reformed. It alone has the right to stand and say, I have made liberty. And this is an historical fact which no man can gainsay.

ii. Then there is the matter of Equality. Equality means that in the eye of the law and of justice there is no difference between man and man. Law and justice know no rich and know no poor : know no sovereign and know no beggar : they only know the man. But equality means more than this. It means not of course that inherent capacity, mental endowment, personal dignity and character are the same in all men; but it means that in the latent, yet actual ideal of humanity, or in the potential yet intrinsic worth which belongs to our nature as human, all men are equal. Within every man there is an ideal latent, perhaps dead and even buried, but still an ideal capable of resurrection: and it is this ideal of humanity in every man which makes the true equality. And whence came the ideal which constitutes what we term equality? It came into the world when this principle was stated:—" There is no respect of persons with God: God is no respecter of persons." That was the first great yet simple formulization of the principle; and the principle lies at the root of all our later social development, making this evident that it is only where you have men equally related to God, God equally related to every man, that you have men made equal.

iii. As with Equality, so with Fraternity. It reposes upon the great faith in the Fatherhood of God and the consequent brotherhood of men. You cannot find any other basis so deep, so broad, so strong as this. And this is the basis Christianity laid, without which the belief in fraternity would never have been, and could not even now continue to be. It is only where men feel as sons of a common Father, that they feel towards each other, however distant in time or space, however dissimilar in race or speech or nationality, as towards brothers. And have you considered the forms in which the Christian religion has helped men to realize their brotherhood? "Who is my neighbour?" asked the lawyer, and Jesus made answer by the parable of the good Samaritan; and ever since, the men who have most loved Christ, have been men who have done into practice the moral of His parable. What did the charities of the early church signify? That a religion had arisen among men that was a religion of brotherhood and mutual helpfulness. What do modern missions signify? That the most cultivated and high-blooded peoples on earth recognize their kinship, and the obligations of their kinship, to the most savage and debased? Science loves to be generous and beneficent, but it cannot be said to pity the savage; knows not what better to do with him than to speculate as to his place in the history of civilization, and as to the causes of his decline and decay under its touch. Commerce likes to discover new peoples and lands, but only that she may find a new market, a field where by more advantageous barter she can increase the riches of the civilized, even though it be by working poverty and ruin to the savage. Certain imperial peoples love to find new scenes for the exercise and display of their imperial genius; but imperial policies only the more deeply divide the sovereign from the subject race. These are not the methods either for creating or expressing fraternity; where the stronger man sees in the weaker only a means for his own instruction, or a source of wealth, or an instrument for his ends, he may use him as a tool, but he will never think of him, feel to him, or act towards him, as a brother. But Christian missions witness to the fact that the Christian religion has accomplished this marvellous feat. It has made civilized man feel that he and the savage are of one blood, that the savage is as dear to God as he is, has as vast capabilities, as boundless promise of being as his own nature can boast. The religion that has created this sense of kinship and duty is the true mother of man's faith in human fraternity.

2. I deeply regret that I must now leave out a large part of what I had meant to say, and shall only ask you to consider whence came the great forces ameliorative and helpful in modern society. Take for example the emancipation of the slave—why accomplished, why prosecuted, by whom and for what reasons ultimately carried through. Were not the men and their motives altogether Christian? Then think of the reform of prisons. Can you forget John Howard and Mrs. Fry, what they were, and what they did? Consider, too, the attempts at criminal reform— ragged schools, reformatories, the varied agencies which wed mercy with justice and reform with penalty. If you look even at the great broad field of war, so dread, so terrible in its destructiveness, what touches it with the gentle spirit of mercy? Why is there the red cross on the white ground? What does it mean but that the minister of mercy is the minister of religion, conscious or unconscious minister perhaps, yet minister still? Had time per-

mitted, I should also have surveyed some of our modern philosophies, especially those that seek to create a religion of humanity, and should have attempted to show that wherever they are creative, energetic, great in their ameliorative impulse, they have borrowed, without acknowledgment, and unconsciously perhaps, but still borrowed from the religion of Christ. This only must I ask you in conclusion to remember: These elements, all of them, need to be gathered into an organic whole, into a living structure, placed in relation to a great throbbing centre. You cannot have sporadic, dismembered, isolated Christian forces, walking up and down the land doing their work: you must bring all into unity, you must centre, converge, weld them into the great central thought, into the mighty living organism. Without Christ, without the Eternal Father, without the living Saviour and the living God, they are impotent, destined to slow, inevitable death. Men and brethren! I speak to you as unto men who love order, who love freedom, who love justice, who love right. What has come to you as a glorious heirloom from the past, a splendid force that has worked out your highest happiness, your best prosperity, your darling principles of hope, claims as its due your strenuous loyalty and noblest thanks. Faith, life, enthusiasm, entire devotion of the spirit, are the simple tribute it deserves.

VI

THE CHRISTIAN RELIGION IN HISTORY AND IN MODERN LIFE

THE lecture of to-night is to deal with religion in the face of to-day, especially so far as it has light to shed upon the great and the vital problems that relate to the welfare and to the well-being of our toiling millions. If religion be what it has been here described as being, it ought to have some light to shed on these problems. It is not the theoretical unbelief of to-day that troubles me; it is its practical ungodliness. The worst denial is not the denial of the name of God, but of the reign of God, and His reign is denied whenever men confess that He is, but live as if He had no kingdom, no law to govern the individual, to be incorporated or realized in the society or the state. Men have been too anxious to limit religion, to keep it as they think to its own province and work, forgetting that the province of religion is the whole man and the whole life of all men. To narrow the sphere or the authority of religion is only a bad way of impugning its truth, a stealthy way of evading its claims. To throw the emphasis from the inward and ethical to the outward and ceremonial is but a more pretentious form of evasion. I confess that I am sick even unto death of what Ruskin has well called the "dramatic Christianity of the organ and the aisle, of dawn-service and twilight revival, gas-lighted and gas-inspired Christianity," and I long with my whole heart to see all our churches become branches of the only true mother-church, the church that is the mother of all our humanities, because the home of all our divinities, the bearer, the living vehicle, of the great purpose, or burden God sent through His Son and by His Spirit to man. If religion were truly interpreted and represented in the living of all Christian men, as it ought to be, I have no fear as to its being believed. It needs but Christian men and churches to be faithful to the mind of Christ to make that mind reign in and over modern men.

Now the aim and purpose of these lectures has been to exhibit religion in its larger aspect, in its wider historical and social significance. There has been no attempt at philosophical or historical apologetics, only at the discovery and exposition of the forces which history has proved to have worked most for our common human good. The faith of Christ is to me the last and highest truth, the worthiest as concerns God, the most reasonable as it relates to man. But though that position be most capable of proof, it is not one that has been here specifically attempted to be proved. I may at some future time make the attempt; for I do not deny the right of inquiry in matters of faith, on the contrary, I hold it a most sacred duty. Truth loves to be searched into, to be inquired after, to have the light of heaven let in upon it from all sides; but truth discloses her presence to none but the pure in mind and heart, to those only who seek her out of sincerity and great love. The man who speaks dishonourably of another's faith does no honour to his own; the man who uses a dishonourable weapon in the battle for the truth dishonours truth, and to dishonour it is to be disowned of the truth, and so to lose it. For what can it do but forsake the man whose soul is forsaken of reverence?

I

1. Our purpose, then, has not been apologetic, but simply historical and expository, an attempt by the help of scientific analysis and comparative criticism to discover those moral and religious forces that have most contributed alike to the individual and common good. And this question was chosen because it seemed at once the most radical and the most relevant to the problems now before the people. The work done for the past has now to be done for the present, and so to-night we shall attempt a further exposition of those principles we have been studying in history in their relation to living man, or simply

to our political, social, industrial questions. Yet it is necessary that we see the relation of our new discussion to our old. Mark, then, the principle which has underlain all our discussions :—Every society is built up on certain great beliefs or ideas. It articulates or expresses these in its institutions, laws, ideals, aims. The beliefs or ideas that underlie the society or state are the truths or beliefs that constitute its religion. As these are, its institutions must be. Find out the ultimate beliefs of a people and you will find out the character of its institutions, or from the study of its institutions you can work back to its fundamental beliefs. Where these beliefs are bad, society cannot be good. Where the fundamental faith is in a might,—that is, in an oppressive, irresistible force,—the institutions will express simply a realized tyranny, a struggle of conflicting forces where the strongest has prevailed.

Look for one moment at certain typical religions. China is remarkable for its ancestral worship. That is its most common and its most ancient worship; but to worship ancestors is so to revere the past as to stand for ever by it. The people who worship their forefathers are the most conservative of peoples; where the father stood, the sons try to stand; departure from the old law is last impiety. So China has been through thousands of years stationary, has hardly known change, and living so, has been persistent, remaining while other more changeful empires pass and decay. Or look at

India. As we have seen, the ultimate thought in the Indian mind is Brahma. Brahma means the universal soul, or life; it is but the equivalent of necessity, the reign of a force that, unresting, runs through all forms of being, one in essence, and necessary in its action, while ever changing its form. In harmony therewith they have conceived Brahma as the universal soul, and thinking of him anthropomorphically, have said: from his head was made the Brahman, the man of the priestly race, from his breast and arms the Kshatriya, the royal and warrior caste, from his legs was made the Vaisya, the yeoman, the farmer, and from his feet were made the Sudras, the toiling class, the lowest caste in the ancient Hindu world. Now, that is a religious theory become a social tyranny. The caste-order is the order of God, and the head has not only the right of commanding the arms and the trunk, and of using the limbs, but of treading ruthlessly on those formed from the feet and lying underneath them. Or take, as before, the ancient empires of the nearer east, Egypt or Assyria. They conceived emperor or king as divine. He owned the nation, all the people were his, and he could do with his own as he pleased, and as he pleased he did with his own. So look how Tiglath-Pileser, Shalmanezer, Sennacherib, Assur-Bani-Pal, and the other Babylonian and Assyrian conquerors, led forth their mighty thousands, threw their armies away in the desert, or at a siege, and cared nothing for the armies they threw away, only for their own purposes or ends. Now contrast with this the past week.[1] Every home in England has thrilled with pain—why? In an African desert a handful of heroic Englishmen was surrounded and assailed by an army of strong and brave Soudanese, and there, in the unequal conflict, 110 of our brothers are said to have perished. And how have we received the news? The thought of those brothers of ours dying there, and no less the thought of the brave barbarians who so strenuously fought and so willingly died for altar and home, is to this people a thought of suffering, brings a sense of personal pain and loss. Now, why do we so value human life, while in the ancient world life was thrown so thoughtlessly away. To ask anew that question is right and necessary, for in it lies the difference between two worlds. You will never build up a free and ordered state, you will never have wealth well distributed, you will never have honour and order, good in their kind, realized, unless you esteem man noble, and esteem all men alike. Here, then is the problem :—high order, waiting on a right idea of man, is in process of being realized now, but was not realized in the old world, nor is realized in any eastern heathenism—why this difference? The answer is the answer that comes back over all the ages; because of what has come through Christ.

[1] Sunday, March 16.—On the Thursday before the battle of *El Teb* had been fought.

2. Let me recall, though but for a moment, the argument of the past lectures. They proceeded, when the question became historical, from this position: all old religions prior to the religion of Israel had no moral character, because no moral deity. Being without moral deities and religions, the nations were not built upon moral principles or for moral ends, but only through despotism or for personal or sectional interests. The coming, through Moses, of the high faith in Jehovah and His law laid the foundation for a new order, made one possible. The order was not a priest's, the order was not a king's, it was God's, and as God's based on His moral law, which expressed His moral nature. It made every man responsible to God directly. It made God govern every man alike. Where God is the common Ruler, the distinction between king and subject may remain on the lower and limited field of the State, but its old absolute character is lost, for on the higher plane, where temporal distinctions disappear in eternal, both stand alike as subjects of God, equal in the eye of His law. The rich and the poor meet together, the Lord is the Maker of them all. And standing equal in the eye of His law, then there is a worth attached to the man, to the single person, to the individual soul, that makes his sufferings, the loss of his life or of his happiness, a crime against God and against the order He instituted. Starting from that rudimentary point, note how the ancient Jewish state was built up. It was built up in order that the will of God,—that is,

His moral law,—might in the relations of man to man reign, and in the action of state and people be realized. Now, the ideas of the Old Testament were taken up and incorporated in the New, but extended into a universalism. God became the Father of all men, loved all men, all men became brethren, the human race one vast family, every unit stood to every other as brother to brother, and the duties enjoined were fraternal duties, the duties of universal neighbourliness and brotherliness. On this great position an entirely new order of the world could be built, an entirely new course and organization of humanity could take place. Man at first did not understand what had come. The old was too strong for the new, out of the ancient religions, out of the ancient state, old forces came into the Christian society and reigned there, yet in spite of these, through the form in which they were incorporated, great Christian truths worked, and worked penetratingly, lovingly, assimilatively, through the whole of society and the life of man. And when later, in a moment of supreme religious fervour, which was also a moment of rare intellectual quickening, the world tried to go back to the nobler primitive thought, then new forces, released and relieved, created higher liberty in the state, purer thought in the life, more equal justice between man and man. And so the new spiritual force has been at work, subordinating the old unto itself, and the humanity that is rising is a humanity distinctively in its basis of Christ, though for God.

II

1. Now, mark, the conclusion of our past discussions is the foundation of our new. The conclusion is this, the great fundamental Christian beliefs, the beliefs as to God, as to man, as to man in relation to God and His purposes, have supplied a new basis for human thought, and so a new foundation for human society; and the society that is being built up on this basis is radically unlike the ancient society. Now, observe, I say is being, I do not say has been, built up. The work is in process. It is not completed, and in the doing of it every man of us ought to bear his part. But while the building proceeds, worked by the hands of men, it is to be in harmony with the beliefs directly created by Christ. These beliefs may be described as, borrowing a word from one of the greatest philosophers, architectonic, that is, they are beliefs that while they construct, regulate the structure, govern it in all its parts and in its ultimate design. Their action has been illustrated in history, for wherever Christ's personal influence has been mightiest and most immediate, there the building has most victoriously proceeded. It has been with Him, in Him, through Him, that all has been done. Did time permit, I would take you a wide survey of the ancient ideals of humanity, and compare them with our own.

I would take you, for example, to the ancestral worship of China, the adoration of heaven, as prescribed and followed by the ancient sages, and would show you this worship making a people that may not move, that lives on in a kind of permanent immobility; or I would take you to the ancient Hindoo ideal as it stands incarnated in the laws of Manu. These laws determine a man's future by his relation to the priestly caste. If a man despises a priest, stands in his way, or uses profane speech of him, he is sentenced to painful punishment, here and hereafter. If a Brahman woman breaks her caste by marriage, there follows degradation for her, and for her offspring, and for their offspring, degradation in ever descending degrees. There we find a whole society fitted into an iron framework, built up, inflexible, immovable, according to the mind of a tyrannical priesthood. Or I would take you to the greater ideas that lie in Plato, in the Republic and in the Laws, already in a way sketched, making the modified Greek Republic possible, yet making a humanity utterly void and mean. He, great as he was, thanked providence that he was born a Greek, and no barbarian, free and no slave. To be a barbarian! It had been better not to have been born than to have had so to speak as to emit sounds that could hardly be held articulate or reasonable speech.

But, now, what is our own modern dream, our ideal vision? All this great humanity forms a mighty family. Man, in all his units, stands the creature of God, His offspring eternally loved by Him, called by Him through love into being. Man as a race is constituted in all his branches a unity through the one God, and is, as an individual, a being who owes duties to every other man, owes duties of good, of service, of truth, of honour, of right, of grace. There is here a notion of man, of humanity, that gives a dignity to the person and a nobility to the race unimagined by the ancients, that makes of human nature a higher thing, and of human life a nobler thing. And I anew affirm, the life we live and know, is, while in all its noble elements the direct creation of Christ, yet at best remains only the promise of what He has still to achieve.

2. Now, I should have liked exceedingly, in the light of our discussions, to have compared these Christian beliefs with certain modern ideas, proposed as substitutes for them, and have judged these beliefs and ideas comparatively. For example, men say, if we could get rid of the human soul and its immortality, how much happier we should be; the belief in a continued being hereafter only makes the here more intolerable. Now one great advantage of the comparative study of religion is this:—Whenever a statement like that is made, you at once turn to places or religions where such things have been realized, look at them, analyze their elements and action, and so discover their intrinsic quality and essential results. Now, there is a

religion that does deny souls, and knows no conscious personal immortality. What of that religion—the religion of Buddha—so far as concerns happiness in this life? It is the apotheosis of misery, the religion that declares that life is not worth living, and that the supreme good is the entire escape from personal being. Observe, where suffering is glorified, is made a sort of deity that devours the very notion of life, the religion instead of saving from pain, is one that arrests progress, that entirely bars secular action, that prevents the highest social forms of life from being realized; and these, precisely, are the results that have followed the religion of Buddha.

Again, there is the notion abroad, clothed, too, in the terms of a very large and audacious philosophy, that we might find in matter or in force a substitute for God, or, at least, the term that could best express the permanent and efficient course of the world we know. Now, note, I will not discuss the question from the metaphysical point of view, otherwise I should ask—pray, how do you know matter, and what may matter be? If you subtract mind and the qualities mind supplies to matter, what of matter may remain, and what of your knowledge of its qualities? A late distinguished thinker, John Stuart Mill, defined matter as the permanent possibility of sensation, but he carefully avoided telling us what the permanent possibility of sensation meant. Does it mean the permanent possibility of force, or does it mean the permanent possibility of mind? Sensation is a mental state, something caused or experienced, derivative therefore and not ultimate; its essential element is the conscious, the perceived, the felt. And so to speak of matter as a permanent possibility of sensation makes it subjective, not objective, that which is known through mind, not capable of definition otherwise than in its terms. Or suppose you take a distinguished physicist, Professor Tyndall, who in a large way in a presidential address to the British Association led us an excursion into a past which he very imperfectly knew, indeed, could not be said to know at all. He there told us— matter has the promise and the potency of every form and quality of life, but when we began to seek after this matter, we were told it is mysterious, an inscrutable power, something utterly unknown. And if we call in the great master of Agnosticism and ask him for his proof that matter or force is the known ultimate, he will tell you that you know it because it resists you. The force within meets resistent forces without, and you know, therefore, matter to be. But, look, take away the force within, and what of the forces without? You must postulate will, or how can you discover or conceive force? you must postulate thought, or how can you find matter or describe what property or quality it has?

But leaving aside the metaphysics, and looking at the question as one concerned merely with a basis for society and state, for an order and law to help the men who work, what then? Well, if matter be the ultimate or causal reality, it means the reign of the mechanical, the necessary, the reign of force, but, mark, when it comes to be applied as a reign of force to life, to the region of social and industrial structure, how does it act? The weakest go to the wall, the strongest survive. All that are feeble perish or are crushed, all that are mighty reign and endure. When it comes to the region of political life, what is the action? The same. Might is the regnant force or power, strength is victor; the king is the person who is mightiest, the one who has subdued all. Translate that into speech for modern times, and it means this: wherever you have most might, the greatest strength and the power to use it, there you have the source of order, the power that reigns, the very reason and essence of government. But what do you call that? Why you call it tyranny, despotism, the hardest, most obdurate and inflexible. Thus from mechanical force, taken as the ultimate datum of consciousness and factor of change, and so as the new basis of social order, we shall have the worst tyranny the world ever saw, tyranny that would throw life away without grudge or care, tyranny that would expel morality, annihilate progress, and make the rich ever richer, the poor ever poorer, marching onward like a mighty law of nature which sets its ruthless foot down on every feeble cause, crushing under it everything that could not by sheer and simple might assert its right to be. That reign would be the ruin of all our noblest order, the loss of our grandest gains.

Now I would it were possible to look at some of the ways of evading this conclusion that have become very fashionable in these recent years. One distinguished thinker wrote lately on "The Religion of the Future," and another not less distinguished thinker described his doctrine as "The Ghost of Religion," and went on to propound the grand Comtean thesis of a religion of humanity, where humanity was the object of worship, and humanity was loved, and served as the modern and natural deity. Now, I have no special care or concern to ask respecting the genesis of Comte's idea of humanity as a great being. But what his disciples think concerning that as a grand new generalization of positive science and philosophy only shows their pathetic innocence as to the actual facts of history and faith. There is a notion of collective humanity far grander than Comte's. There is a notion of humanity which makes it one immense family, a family of God; makes it one immense society, a society of sons who are brothers—one immense household, where every member is bound to serve the others, that by this service he may the better serve his own Eternal Father. That was a grander idea than Comte's, penetrated throughout by a principle of tremendous energy, which could build up and organize the race into a vital unity. His is but a headless humanity, an aggregation of atoms, no living organism. It rises, he knows not whence, moves across the earth, and vanishes, he knows not whither. But this is a humanity lifted into eternity, living in the life of God, a humanity loved of God, redeemed of Him, intended to be perfected in all its parts and in all its members, that it may live in holiest fellowship with Him. Every man who does good unto the least of men, does it unto God : practical beneficence in time, the love that suffers unto the saving of man is the noblest service of the Eternal. That is a sublime idea. In its presence the positive notion is indeed the veriest ghost of religion, spectral, impalpable, impotent, save to the visionary who sees it.

3. Let us come back, then, to our position, though only that we may re-affirm it the more strongly; the Christian religion is by virtue of its very nature creative of a new mankind, constitutive of a new society. Its fundamental principles are architectonic, supply at once the basis and the regulative ideal for the renewed humanity. It is meant to create a perfect state through perfect men, and it certainly does not mean to leave its renewed men under the control of an unspiritual order. Do not think that I am speaking new things, they are things as old as Christianity. At its birth our religion was possessed of a divine ambition, for it was inspired by divine truth, and articulated a divine design. Christ's coming was no accident; it had been purposed from eternity. Nature and man had been alike founded on and by Him. So one apostle said : "All things were made

by Him, and without him was not anything made that was made." He was "the true Light" and "the true Life," and there was no true life, no true light, in the world that did not come from Him. Another apostle said, "By Him were all things created that are in heaven and earth;" and "in Him all things hold together," stand in order or system. As He is the source, He is also the means and end, for through Him and to Him are all things. And so He is represented, not only as the Head of the Church, but as the One in whom all things, both which are in heaven and on earth, are to be gathered together, summed up, or made into a unity. Now ideas of that kind signify a large faith, the faith that all things were created and constituted in Christ, that as He is, on the one side, the image of the invisible God, so He is, on the other, the ideal or regulative principle of the visible creation. Applied to our present subject this means, that Christ was intended to be, in the fullest sense, a Saviour, not only of the individual, but also of society, making the man new, but doing it that He might renew mankind. Within Him were the energies needed to create a perfect order, a holy society, a humanity that should articulate the Creator's ideal. The work that He came to do was to reconcile man to God, to bring alike our nature as persons and the order in which we lived and worked into harmony with the will of God. And so He was the Son of Man who made man into the Son of God, the Redeemer, delivering from sin, the Saviour, bringing into life eternal. The grand thing about His mission was its positive aspect —His saving man, and the completeness of His salvation. The Christian religion had indeed an awful sense of sin, a deep sense of misery; but that is only the reverse side of its majestic sense of God, its sublime idea of man. It is because it conceives man to be so great that it feels his sin to be so terrible; it is because it conceived man to be so near of kin to God that it allowed him such susceptibility to suffering, such faculty of gain, such capacity for loss. But as was the loss, so is the salvation. It is not finished when a man is forgiven, or has obtained peace with God; it is completed only when Christ is all and in all—that is, when humanity has been built up in all its parts and regulated in all its relations by the ideal of love and sonship that had lived from eternity in the bosom of God.

III

You see, then, there are, as I conceive it, architectonic principles in the religion of Christ; and it is the simplest and most rudimentary of these that I wish to apply to our political, social, and industrial questions. This is only a small branch of an immense subject; but I am anxious so to handle it as to illustrate for our time the significance of the Christian religion. These questions will sufficiently test its right to be the organizing principle of the noblest society, and the regulative law of the truest life.

1. Our political, social, and industrial questions, while distinct, are so related as to form an organic whole. You cannot touch one without touching all the rest; the body politic is as sensitive and as much an organic unity, as the body of the living man. Our political questions concern man as a citizen, with the rights and duties proper to one; they touch his relation to the state, and the state's to him. Our social questions concern man's place and functions, duties and rights, as a part of a mighty organism, whose members are human beings; and view organism and members in their mutual relations and obligations, as affected by and affecting each other. Our industrial questions concern the creation, accumulation and distribution of wealth, regard man as producer, distributer, consumer, as a being capable of toil, yet needing rest, with capital, land or money or skill, that he wishes to lend or sell, that he may obtain or create a wealthier condition of being. These provinces of thought and action, though distinct, are inseparable. Every question raised in the one has its correlative in the other, and the point of unity is man. He is the living and sensitive atom that thrills with pleasure or writhes in pain with every current that passes through the body, political social or industrial.

i. Now, if we are to consider the Christian religion in relation to these questions, we must do so in the light of some simple principles, yet they must be those of the architectonic order   Now, our simplest, yet mightiest, principle is given us in the idea of God as manifested in Christ, the Father as declared by the only begotten Son. What was the purpose of God relative to man, alike in creation and redemption? His good—his highest good. Man may have as his chief end to glorify God, but God finds His glory —and in the light of Christ's words and work it is seen to be the only godlike glory possible—in promoting the good of man. As He intends that, so He means that all the godlike energies in the universe shall contribute to it. But what is for man the chief good? It consists in two elements, in the union, as the moralist would say, of virtue and pleasure, or, as the religious man, of holiness and happiness. In the state of perfect good, virtue is completely happy, holiness has attained beatitude. But what does this involve? The perfect man, but also the perfect state, the state ordered and administered in perfect righteousness, where the virtue within has its mirror and reflection in the order without. We could not have the highest good with vice, for it is hateful, envious, miserable, seeks only to get pleasure, loves only to inflict pain; so virtue is necessary, the holiness that loves to do the best and obey the holiest. Nor could the highest good be found in a vicious state; the good, the perfect man may live there, but the evil without would hate him, and he could not love it; there might be the joy of conflict, but there could not be the highest joy, the joy of perfect harmony, of the constant motion that is constant rest.

In order then to the chief good, the righteous man must live in a righteous state; virtue within and virtue without must dwell together in beautiful and holy unity. But if God means that each person realize the chief good, what ideal does He set before us for society? This: that the individuals composing it shall, every one of them, be perfectly virtuous or perfectly holy, and that the state into which they are organized shall in every respect be perfectly ordered and perfectly righteous, an altogether good and holy state. No less an ideal as respects man, on the one hand, and society, on the other, can satisfy the Christian idea of God.

ii. Now this, you will confess, is no mean ideal, and rests on no contemptible or ignoble principle. We may be an infinite distance from its realization, but it is a matter of infinite importance that we feel ourselves held bound to work for it and to travel with our faces towards it; making, while we do so, the present better, and bringing the golden future more near. To have conceived this ideal is to feel man ennobled, is to have gained a brighter view of the prospects and possibilities of our kind. Yet on what does it rest? On the notion of God as a Spiritual Father and Sovereign on the one hand, and, on the other, on the notion of man as His son and subject, bound to be obedient to Him and to realize His order. Now let me ask you a simple question—Do you know any principle so able as this to do large and generous justice to the noblest possibilities of order and progress in the state, and of happiness and manhood in the man? The idea of humanity, you say; but Christ created the idea of humanity, and divorced from Him it is but a bastard idea, at once emasculated and depraved. What value is there in an idea that is but an impotent abstraction, that gives no moral source, no moral sovereign, and no moral end to human life, either individual or collective? If you renounce this Christian principle, where will you find a basis for your social structure? for a basis you must find; and remember this—as is the basis, such must the structure be. Suppose we inquire at the men best able to advise us in this matter, really representative and creative thinkers, who have attempted to find another than the Christian basis for society. We shall find that they confirm the truth of the argument we have before pursued. There is Hobbes, an honest and courageous Materialist, who did not fear to deduce from his first principles their rigorous logical results. To believe in matter as the ultimate ground and cause of all things, is to believe in the supremacy and sufficiency of force, and in a conflict of forces the strongest must prevail. Carry out that doctrine in the arena of politics, and you have Hobbes's theory, the most forcible man is king. The original state was a state of war, that is, a conflict of opposing forces; order came from the victory of the mightiest, which means that the strongest force prevailed; the victor became the sovereign, his will became the law, made the right, instituted, constituted the order and relations in which the people lived. That is a clear and intelligible theory, massive in its simplicity, rigorous in its consistency, but what does it mean? The most absolute tyranny, despotism unrelieved. Let us try another. Rousseau hated Materialism, but wished to find a social doctrine that should, apart from Christianity, secure to all men their natural rights. And what did he propose? The theory of a "Social Contract." Men met together and agreed on the conditions on which they would associate; signed, as it were, a pre-historical contract of co-operation, which concluded, they laid aside their isolation or individualism, and combined in a society or state. Those who kept to the contract were the lawful citizens, those who broke it by claiming too much or by doing too little, were the guilty. But, mark, a society held together by a covenant or bond is an artificial society; the bond, too, is in this case an historical fiction, made all the falser by making the savage the ideal or standard for the civilized man. Humanity bound to fulfil an imaginary primitive bond, has lost at once the rights of the present and the inspiration of the future, and renounced the idea of order and the hope of progress. Again, David Hume, subtlest and most consistent of Sceptics, always, as we saw, Sceptic-like opposed to the highest human liberty, said, "Government has no other object or purpose than the distribution of justice, or, in other words, the support of the twelve judges." And why? "Every man must be supposed a knave," with no other end but his private interest, which he must be prevented gratifying at the expense of the public. So government in its last analysis is a plan which a multitude of knaves have adopted, if not for making each other honest, yet for keeping by fear of punishment dishonesty within bounds. Could you conceive a more miserable basis for politics, or one that did more injustice alike to the idea and the history of man? It rests on a notion of him so mean that it bemeans everything; it appeals to the meanest motives in man, and makes of him a creature who has interests, but no duties, who may need protection, but can exercise no rights. It is small wonder that a system so based should have had no room for liberty, no idea of moral order, or faith in the higher progress and well-being of man.

Now what, in opposition to these, does the Christian religion offer as its grand fundamental principle in politics? Its idea of God and its ideal of man, viewed in their mutual or reciprocal relations. It says: "God is the father of man, man is the child of God. He wills every man's good, and every man ought to attain the good He wills; what is possible to the individual is possible to the society. He is capable of being virtuous, it is capable of being in all its order and relations righteous. The ideal that is in him, it is bound to accept, and to work for its realization ; the ideal that is before it, he is bound to regard as his own, and strenuously to do his utmost to secure its embodiment. The law of the state ought to be in harmony with God's will, and so such as shall intend and promote the good of all its citizens ; the conduct of the citizen ought to be governed by the same will, and seek at once the reign of righteousness in the state, and its realization in the individual. To the good man the law of God is absolute and universal, a law alike for persons and peoples, designed to govern all states, and be obeyed of all men. If, then, in civil life, there lie a wrong, Christian politics ought to redress the wrong ; if in social life inequalities or agencies that hinder the distribution or creation of good, Christian society ought to move against them. Religion cannot be satisfied till the ideal of the perfect man in the perfect state be realized."

2. You see, then, that the Christian religion supplies us for all civil and social questions with constructive and regulative principles of the noblest kind. In their light politics become the science of working out a perfect order in which every man shall achieve virtue and attain happiness, that is, realize the ideal of humanity latent within him. But I can only state the principles : it is impossible to apply them in detail to the questions of legislation and government. Yet, though only by way of illustration, let us glance at a question or two.

i. And first, as being most germane to our subject, as concerns our poor. Religion does not regard poverty as a normal state, rather as one that ought not to be. Where charity is needed, it is a noble thing to be charitable, and charity was one of the most characteristic creations of Christ. But there is something better than charity, a state where it is not needed, where all men are able and willing to earn their own livelihood, and enjoy what they have earned. Now religion deals with poverty primarily as a matter of persons, and it is through persons alone that it can be overcome. Laws may mitigate its severity, but its removal depends on the kind and quality of persons composing the state. The better a man is made, the better a worker he is, the fitter an agent for the creation of wealth, and the expulsion of poverty. It is the worthless that waste ; worth is productive and distributive. It makes for itself, but loves also to share with others. Now the Christian religion in making good men, makes good workers, self-respectful, independent, fore-thoughtful ; in honouring work as no other religion does, it dignifies the workman. Yet, if misfortune or disaster comes, there is no spirit so tender, so helpful as the Christian. It will not leave to perish, but helps that it may save. And its charity is not of the legal order, hurting where it helps ; but of the merciful order, which is twice blessed, blessing him that gives and him that takes. So our religion works at once to prevent poverty, and where it must be, is qualified so to ameliorate its action that it shall not deprave the man. A people wholly Christian could not be poor.

ii. Another question, partly political and partly social, is the one now being so much discussed as to the housing of the poor. Has religion, as here construed, any light to shed on it? It insists, in an equal degree, on the person and his conditions being good. What makes a person bad or compels him to live under bad conditions, conditions unfavourable to moral and physical health, is a religious wrong. Thus, if a man owns a rookery, and makes it his business to let houses unfit for human homes, he must be held guilty of crime before God and against man. Religion binds a man to follow no profession, to exercise no craft, save one promotive of human wellbeing. If it be profitable while injurious, the profits only the more add to the sin, because emphasizing its reckless selfishness. Men must live, but our means of living must be honourable to be approved of religion. And see here its value as the power for making right persons. Only mean men are capable of doing mean things, while noble men alone are equal to noble deeds. Let a man be possessed of the spirit of Christ, the charity that seeketh not her own, that seeks generously the good of every neighbour, and to him the miserable greed that can make money out of the poverty or destitution of man is not only impossible, but unholy and abominable.

iii. We have a third question, or rather set of

questions, connected with what is perhaps the saddest of all our modern problems, what men call the social evil. There is no deeper or viler sore in the heart of society, though I may not speak of it here as it needs to be spoken of. Yet it is an evil on which religion has a pre-eminent right to be heard, while also lying under solemnest obligations to speak. To it man can never be a mass of organized lusts, whose indulgence is to be tempered by prudence, for to it man at his noblest is most continent. Of all humankind, there is none poorer, no wretch more contemptible or base, than the lustful man, capable of working grief to a woman, heedless of her sorrow or shame, her sad, blighted, lost womanhood ; capable of hiring for the indulgence of his bestial passions a poor fallen creature, forgetful that even wrecked womanhood ought to be sacred to the man who is a son, and had, or has, a mother. Could I compass it, I should make every such lustful man a man to be punished, for there is no greater foe to social good, no force that so threatens the peace of every virtuous home. Yet, how is he to be reached, how dealt with ? Not by outer laws simply, not by external restraints, not by preaching the prudence that tempers passion only that it may be the longer indulged ; but by filling him with a spirit too great, too honourable, too noble, too full of chivalrous chastity to feel the passion of lust, or the fascination of base desires. And only one supreme love has been able to accomplish that. The love of Christ has been the love of purity, both in man and woman, the love of God has ever been love of chastity, binding man to too noble issues to allow him to stain his manhood with impurity, or to deprave womanhood by his passions. Were that love to reign in society, we should soon see realized the highest social good.

iv. But now we must come, though for the briefest glance, to our Industrial Questions. One thing Religion cannot do—it cannot lose sight of man as a living, reasonable soul; but what Religion cannot do, Political Economy did. Its founder, Adam Smith, was not responsible for that. The author of the "Wealth of Nations" was also the author of a system of Moral Philosophy. And do you know its peculiar doctrine? It was based on feeling, on sympathy; it was your feeling for man, your sympathy with him, that made you approve what promoted his good, disapprove what hindered it. But the men who followed Adam Smith forgot his "Theory of Moral Sentiments," and dealt with wealth as if the factors of its creation and distribution had been mere tools, instruments, pieces of mechanism. You know Sismondi's question to Ricardo:—"What then! is wealth everything? is man nothing?" And wealth was everything to the political economist, man valued only in relation to it. And it was this indifference to men that made political economy to Carlyle, Adam Smith's great countryman, the "dismal science." But who creates? who distributes? who accumulates wealth? Who but man? And man is greater than any product, or any process of production, or even all the creations of his hand or genius. And no product is good that does not help to make the producer happier and better; and only as the producers are improved can the products go on improving. And so the science that does not take men into account is no true science of wealth. For what is wealth? A state of weal. The common wealth is the state of common weal. And what is that? The state of good to all. Now wealth is not money, but what constitutes man's weal; it is the well-being of the living. The only wealth of nations is the weal of the peoples; to be rich in persons, rich in the varied elements that make life good to all, is for a nation to have wealth, and to be wealthy. Here, as elsewhere, persons are supreme. Give us persons of the right order, producers, consumers, capitalists, labourers, and all other things will be added—they will adjust themselves into an order promotive of the common good. Treat all questions in industry as questions in religion, and it is certain that those great problems which perplex the present will become problems solved.

(1) But, to select an example or two, take our problems as to land. There are no questions men speak more of to-day. Yet here the supreme thing is the good of the people. All legislation relative to land ought to have that good prominently in view. There is no law of God, there ought to be no law of

man, that so favours the man who owns property in land as to enable him to dispossess the people. He owns it for their good. Even where his rights are recognized, and I recognize them most soundly, he is still, in his very rights, trustee of a great national possession, not for his own weal simply, but for the common good. The rights of property concern a class, and are based on fulfilled duties, which concern the whole people. I am come of a long race of farmers, and love the soil. My grandfather owned a little farm of a hundred odd acres, and he farmed the land he owned. One who loved him as became a daughter used to tell how once, in the corn-law times, when the proprietors cried, " Let us have more protection," the great lord of the neighbourhood came to visit him, and to ask him to sign a petition, praying that still higher duties might be imposed ; and the old man said, " No ! I will not sign." " What ! not sign ? It will enhance the value of your land." " Sir," was the reply, " I will never enhance the value of my land at the expense of the people's food." And he there stated the great principle of religion in the matter. He was a religious man, and as such known and revered all round, and he only thus expressed in a practical article the faith by which he lived. The land was meant to serve the people's good whilst maintaining him. Without it the people cannot live, on it the people have a right to live, and so it can become no man's absolute possession, to be done with as he wills. The rights of property in land, pushed to their last legal limit, might easily become a more oppressive and disastrous tyranny than the divine right of kings to govern wrong ; but the principle alike of the Old and New Testament,—the land is for the people, their possession before the Lord,—limits and defines these rights. The people have not lost their rights in the land by ownership becoming personal ; nay, have only, in a sense, the more fully secured and affirmed them. Communal was exchanged for personal ownership, that through personal responsibilities and action the riches of the soil might be the more increased and extensively distributed. It happened not that all the rights might be concentrated on the head of the possessor, but that all the capabilities of the possession might be developed and diffused. Unless this result follow, personal ownership may become a public wrong, and what has become that may become an evil not to be borne. Trusts faithfully discharged are rights firmly secured ; personal ownership held and exercised for the public good is the only ownership above the need, and so above the fear, of change.

(2) But these are only general religious and Christian principles applied to an economical question, and all that is here possible is to state them. Now this statement ought to lead up to other and varied questions, especially those connected with capital and labour. Now, if this question were approached from the same point of view as one of mutual duties, which imply and recognize mutual rights, how simple it would

become! Where a man works as a religious man to God, he will do it, not as for wage, but as best effort for noblest purpose. Then his ambition will not be to do as little and get as much as he can, but to do the best his skill and energies will allow. Where the employer is religious, he will recognize that he has duties he owes to his workmen, and his ambition will be not to deal with them as "hands," machines that differ from his engines only in being more unstable and irregular in their action, but as souls, to be loved as such, and handled as rational and responsible and sensitive men. If your questions are determined as questions between men who have great moral obligations both in working and employing work, the mutual duties will solve and unite where mutual interests only embitter and divide. But the supreme necessity is here, as elsewhere, the order of persons religion has created and can create. Men who seek each other's good will harmoniously promote each other's weal. Men who believe that they constitute a brotherhood before God will do generously by each other in all questions of economical and industrial relations.

There are also other questions, such as those connected with amusements for the people—which I could have liked to notice, but must leave alone. This question of amusements is one that requires wise methods of solution, for there is nothing we have more need to do than to make life a little more beautiful, fuller of promise and gladness for labouring men. We all ought to feel that a people has a right to be happy, and happy all good men will seek to make them. But all I can say is, let the great moral principles of religion be expressed in our economical methods and laws, and we shall be sure to realize the highest and most beneficent state of being.

My hope for the future is in the ideal of Christ. My hope for man is in a more perfect and complete embodiment of the Christian religion. When I look abroad and see the disintegrative agencies that are hard at work, the one thing I am anxious to do is to bring the great constructive, the great architectonic principles of our Christian faith into relation with life and action. Every Christian principle embodied in law or society, every Christian deed accomplished in industry, helps on the happier time. I have come for these six nights out of my own study in obedience to no call but the call of duty as my conscience apprehended it, to speak to you, my Fellow-townsmen, on matters that are alike to you and me matters of the most vital and transcendent interest, whether as men who work in time or men destined to live in eternity.

I have endeavoured to show you the principles which have done most for humanity in the past; and to make manifest to you, that if in this living present we are to have real and highest welfare, a wealthier state and wealthier men, because men who have realized their manhood's highest state and truest weal, then we must be men more and more baptized into Christ, possessed of His truth, inspired by His love. Then when so inspired, working the work of time as in eternity, building on this earth a city, meant to be the great city of God, we shall hand on to a brightening future the nearer fulfilment of the promise which came to the ages through Jesus Christ our Lord.

THE END

www.ingramcontent.com/pod-product-compliance
Lightning Source LLC
Chambersburg PA
CBHW070239230426
43664CB00014B/2353